A Fan's Guide
Football Grounds
Scotland

Duncan Adams

D1556618

Ian Allan
PUBLISHING

First published 2006

ISBN (10) 0 7110 3188 6
ISBN (13) 978 0 7110 3188 3

© Duncan Adams 2006

Published by Ian Allan Publishing

an imprint of Ian Allan Publishing Ltd, Hersham,
Surrey KT12 4RG.
Printed in England by Ian Allan Printing Ltd,
Hersham, Surrey KT12 4RG.

Code: 0608/C

Visit the Ian Allan Publishing website at
www.ianallanpublishing.com

Front cover, top: Hampden Park.

Front cover, middle: East Fife.

Front cover, bottom: Dundee United.

Back cover, top: Falkirk

Back cover, bottom: Stranraer

Contents

Introduction

Welcome to *A Fan's Guide: Football Grounds – Scotland*. This book covers every ground in the Scottish Premier League, the three Scottish Football Leagues and the national football venue, Hampden Park. Inside you will find a host of information useful to the travelling supporter. Not only are there practical details, such as directions to the grounds, but other information to make your day more enjoyable, such as pub recommendations. There is also of course a number of excellent colour photos of all the grounds themselves.

Not much has been happening recently in terms of the development of the Scottish grounds in terms of new building and redevelopment. The Falkirk Stadium has been the only new stadium to be built and extended in recent years and following on from the club's success a new third stand is on the horizon. Perhaps the biggest change to affect football fans in Scotland has happened outside the grounds with the 'No Smoking Legislation' passed by the Scottish Parliament, which became effective in March 2006. Affecting smoking in public places and in the workplace, smoking has now been effectively banned from all Scottish Football Grounds. So not only can you not get an alcoholic drink inside the ground, but you also can't smoke either. Let's hope that the excitement of the football makes up for it!

The guide has been compiled based on not only my personal visits to the grounds but the feedback of many supporters who have visited them in recent seasons, giving an all-round independent view. Without feedback this book would not have been possible, so a big thank you to everyone who has contributed.

Although I have strived to make sure that every detail is as up to date as it can be, things can change over the course of a season. For example, a pub will close or another open, so please bear this in mind. I hope you find this guide useful and informative. But remember this is only a guide and should be treated as such. If you find that things have changed, feel that you can give better directions or provide useful additional information then please e-mail me at duncan@scottishgrounds.co.uk. Remember, this guide is *for* football fans, *by* football fans, so feel free to have your say. Wherever possible I will strive to include your comments in future editions.

The guide does not cover disabled facilities within the grounds as I feel that currently such information is better covered by other sources. This is something that I will look to address in future editions. Most wheelchair places need to be booked in advance of the match with the individual clubs concerned, of which the telephone numbers are listed within the guide.

For the latest updates to the Guide please visit www.scottishgroundguide.co.uk.

Author

This book is dedicated to my father John Adams, who sadly passed away recently in Glasgow. He first took me to see a game in 1970 (in which the legendary George Best played) and his general interest in football influenced me, in that I have always enjoyed watching football across different levels and at different venues. From 100,000 attendances at Hampden Park for a game against England, to visiting Wembley in 1977 for another England v Scotland match (and no I don't still have any of the Wembley pitch as a memento!), to friendlies, lower league football, schoolboy internationals and even Sunday League games. So from an early age I was hooked on the game and its grounds.

I have come a long way since then and covered many miles and spent probably more money than I would care to add up in visiting grounds across the country watching our beloved game. I still very much enjoy 'travelling away' and watching football at different grounds and stadia. But we should not forget the most important element in football is us, the fans; without the fans it would not be the game that it is.

I hope you enjoy the book and that it will improve your away trips, as well as perhaps whetting the appetite to visit a ground that you hadn't thought about visiting before.
Duncan Adams
August 2006

Special Thanks

To Owen Pavey for providing a number of great photographs, plus thanks to Matthew Day and Jean Francois Foxhall for their photos of Dunfermline and Hibernian respectively. Thanks also to Thomas Mapfumo of European Football Statistics for providing the average attendance information; please visit his website at www.european-football-statistics.co.uk. I am also indebted to Simon Inglis and his book *The Football Grounds Of Great Britain* for some of the historical information contained within this guide. Thanks also to Ian Dewar, an exiled Nottingham Forest fan in Canada, for rewriting parts of the guide so that it became immensely more readable. And lastly to my wife, Amanda, for her unquestioning support and patience in my ground-visiting travels and while putting this book together.

Aberdeen

Pittodrie Stadium

Ground Name: Pittodrie Stadium
Capacity: 22,199 (all seated)
Address: Pittodrie Street, Aberdeen, AB24 5QH
Telephone No: 01224-650-400
Fax No: 01224-644-173
Ticket Office: 01224-631-903
Stadium Tours: 01224-650-400
Pitch Size: 110 x 72 yards
Year Ground Opened: 1899
Undersoil Heating: Yes
Club Nickname: The Dons
Home Kit Colours: Red & White

Official Web Site:
www.afc.co.uk

Unofficial Websites:
Re Final Fanzine - www.redfinal.com
Red Ultras - www.redultras.net

■ What's The Ground Like?
At one end of the ground is the newest and largest stand, the impressive-looking Richard Donald Stand, named after a former Club Chairman. It was opened in 1993 and replaced what was known as the Beach End. This is two-tiered with a row of executive boxes running across the middle. There is a particularly large lower tier, with a smaller upper tier and overall this stand tends to dwarf the others around it. The other end is a much smaller older single-tiered stand called the Merkland Stand. On one side is the old Main Stand, originally built in 1925. As you would expect from an older stand, it has a fair few supporting pillars running along the front of it. Opposite is a large single-tiered cantilever stand, called the South Stand. The corner between this and the Merkland Stand is filled with seating, but this area is the only uncovered area of the ground.

■ Future Ground Developments
After abandoning the proposal to build a new stadium at Bellefield, the Club are now talking to Aberdeen City Council about the possibility of building in partnership a new community stadium in the North Beach area of the city. The proposals at the moment are only that, but if they do make it off the drawing board then a state of the art stadium would be built, which would include a retractable roof, the first ever to be used at any league ground. Pittodrie would be sold off for residential redevelopment.

What Is It Like For Visiting Supporters?

Away fans are housed on the one side of the South Stand. Up to 4,500 supporters can be accommodated in this part of the ground although the normal allocation is around 2,500). Peter Llewellyn adds 'there is normally an excellent atmosphere within Pittodrie, although it is sometimes lacking for the smaller games'. I think Pittodrie gets the vote as one of the most coldest grounds in Britain. Even in spring the biting breeze off the North Sea which is only a few hundred yards away from the perimeter of the ground, can go right through you. Outside look out for the granite entrance to the Merkland Family Stand. Erected in 1928 they celebrate Aberdeen being known as the 'Granite City'.

Where To Drink?

There are not that many pubs nearby, so consider drinking in the city centre before moving onto the ground. Scott McKenzie informs me; 'The nearest bar to the ground is the Broad Hill bar at the back of the Richard Donald Stand, but unfortunately this has a big sign up saying "home support only", although it hasn't always been that way. Next closest are the three Golf Clubs, all of whom operate a signing in/membership type thing, which some away fans do take advantage of and the atmosphere is invariably friendly. If travelling by coach, then all coaches are parked on the beach boulevard, which is close to a bar called The Saltoun, which is popular with away fans. Otherwise there are plenty of bars to choose from in the city centre'.

How To Get There & Where To Park?

The ground is located in the North part of the city (close to Old Aberdeen) and near to the coast line. It is close to the A956.

From The South:
Follow the A90 towards Aberdeen. Just south of Aberdeen join the A956. Keep on the A956 through Aberdeen and eventually you will come to Pittodrie over on your right. Turn right into Pittodrie Street for the ground.

From The North:
Follow the A956 into Aberdeen. You will reach Pittodrie over on your left. Turn left into Pittodrie Street for the ground.

From The West:
Follow the A96 into Aberdeen. At the large roundabout with the A978 turn left into Machar Drive (A978). Proceed along the A978 and then turn right onto the A956 (King Street). Pittodrie Street and the ground is the 5th turning on the left.

There is a large car park at the ground but this is for pass holders only. There is though a fair amount of street parking in side streets and on the Esplanade along the sea front, which is on the other side of the golf course.

By Train

Aberdeen train station is over two miles from the ground and is quite a walk (around 25-30 mins). Best to jump in a taxi up to the ground. However, if you want to brave the walk:

Upon leaving the station turn left and walk across the bridge and then turn right. This brings you into Union Street, where you should walk down until its end, where you will reach Castle Gate. Home supporters should bear left into King Street (A956) and continue down this street before turning right into Merkland Road for the ground. Away supporters should proceed through the Castle Gate and into Park Street. This street eventually becomes Golf Road and you will come to Pittodrie on your left. Thanks to Tom Widdows for providing the directions.

Local Rivals

Although not local, Glasgow Rangers.

Admission Prices

Home Fans:

Main Stand:
Adults £26,
Concessions £18
Under 12's £10

Richard Donald Stand (padded centre seats):
Adults £21,
Concessions £15
Under 12's £8

Richard Donald Stand (other areas):
Adults £20,
Concessions £15

South Stand:
Adults £21,
Concessions £15
Under 12's £8

Merkland Family Stand:
Adults £16,
Concessions £8,
Under 12's £5*
Family Tickets: 2 Adults + 2 Concessions £40*

Away Fans:

South Stand:
Adults £20,
Concessions £15

* Please note that family and under 12 tickets must be purchased from the Customer Services Department.

■ Programme & Fanzine
Official Programme £2.50
Ten Men Went To Mow (10MWTM) £1

■ Record Attendance
45,061 v Heart Of Midlothian,
Scottish Cup, March 3rd 1954.

■ Average Attendance
2005-2006: 12,728 (Premier League)

■ Stadium Tours
The Club offer tours of the ground on weekday mornings. These must be booked in advance by calling the Club on: 01224-650-400. The tours are free of charge!

■ Did You Know?
That in 1978 Pittodrie was the first football league ground in Britain to become all seater.

Ground Name: Celtic Park
Capacity: 60,832 (all seated)
Address: 18 Kerrydale St, Glasgow, G40 3RE
Telephone No: 0141-556-2611
Fax No: 0141-551-8106
Ticket Office: 0141-551-8653
Ticket Office Fax No: 0141-551-4223
Stadium Tours: 0141 551 4308
Pitch Size: 105m x 68m
Year Ground Opened: 1892
Undersoil Heating: Yes
Club Nickname: The Bhoys
Home Kit Colours: Green & White Hoops

Official Web Site:
www.celticfc.net

Unofficial Websites:
Jinky Soars - www.jinkysoars.co.uk
Celtic Paradise- www.celtic-paradise.co.uk
Bhoyzone - www.bhoyzone.net

■ What's The Ground Like?

Celtic Park (although known to many fans by the name of the Parkhead area in which it is situated) is simply a massive stadium that can be seen from miles around. Three quarters of the ground have been redeveloped in recent years greatly improving the overall look. The ground is totally enclosed, with the three new sides being two-tiered. The lower tiers of these stands are huge and come up to roughly the same height as the older Main (South) Stand which is also two-tiered, just showing how large they are. The upper tiers of the new North Stand does have a few supporting pillars, which may obstruct your view (the club do however issue reduced price tickets for those seats effected). The Main Stand is unusual as it has a large roof, most of which is translucent, which makes it look quite striking. The translucency helps keep the pitch in good condition. A television gantry is also suspended from beneath its roof. However with the Main Stand being far smaller then the other sides, the ground looks a little imbalanced. Still if this was to be redeveloped at some point in the future then I'm sure Celtic Park would be in the running for the best club ground in Britain. However, I understand that this may be some time off as the Main Stand is a listed building. There are also two large video screens suspended from beneath the roof at either end of the ground. The quality of the image shown on these screens are superb. Another unusual aspect of the ground is that it has a number of seats that can be heated in cold weather.

David Murphy adds; 'A poll undertaken by BBC Radio 5 Live in 2003, resulted in Celtic Park being voted as the most 'atmospheric sports venue (note, not just football) in the UK'. The stadium has also

been nicknamed 'Paradise' by the Celtic fans.

■ What Is It Like For Visiting Supporters?

Away fans are housed in the lower corner of the Lisbon Lions Stand at one end of the ground.

The views of the playing action and the facilities provided within this stand are excellent, although it should be noted that there are a number of restricted view seats in the away section, for which the club charge a lower admission fee. There are also betting facilities available within the ground. The atmosphere within Celtic Park is superb and it is a great stadium to watch football in. As most games are normally sold out, make sure that you have a match ticket before you travel.

■ Where To Drink?

As would be expected most bars around the Parkhead area, are partisan & particularly busy. It is probably best to drink in the city centre beforehand. However, most of these bars will not serve fans wearing football colours.

■ How To Get There & Where To Park?

The ground is on the East side of Glasgow on the A74 (London Road).

■ From The South:

Stay on the M74 until its end and then continue into Glasgow on the A74. You will come to the ground after about a mile and a half on your right.

■ From The North:

M80 then onto the A80 towards Glasgow and then join the M73 South. At the end of the M73 join the M74 northbound. Stay on the M74 until its end and then continue into Glasgow on the A74. You will come to the ground after about a mile and a half on your right.

■ From The East:

Leave the M8 at Junction 8 and follow the M73 South. At the end of the M73 join the M74 northbound. Stay on the M74 until its end and then continue into Glasgow on the A74. You will come to the ground after about a mile and a half on your right.

There is plenty of street parking to be had, especially in the side streets off the London Road going down towards the A74. Don't be surprised though, as you get out of your car, that some kid appears uttering the words 'mind yer car mister?'

■ By Train

Glasgow Central & Queens Street railway stations are around a 30-minute walk away from the ground. Probably best to jump in a taxi (about £5). Otherwise if you arrive at Glasgow Central you can take a local train to Dalmarnock station which is about a ten-minute walk away from the ground. Paul Boyd provides the following directions to the ground; 'As you come out of the station entrance,

urn right and proceed to the end of the road.
urn left into Dalmarnock Road and proceed up to
he traffic lights at the junction with Mill Street.
urn right at those lights into Mill Street and
roceed all the way along Mill Street until you
each the traffic lights at London Road (at the
unction with the Police Station). From there, you
urn right and Celtic Park is around 250 yards up
he road on the left hand side'.

Local Rivals
Rangers.

Admission Prices
The club operate a category system of games, so
hat the most popular games are priced more then
others.

Adults £23-£31,
Concessions £14-£23

n addition there are a number of 'restricted view'
tickets available, which on an adult ticket are £3
cheaper, then the price quoted above.

Programme & Fanzines
Official Programme £2.
More Than 90 Minutes Fanzine: £2.
Not The View Fanzine: £1.50.

Record Attendance
92,000 v Glasgow Rangers, 1938.

Average Attendance
2005-2006: 58,105 (Premier League)

Stadium Tours
The Club offer regular tours of the stadium, which
cost £8.50 for adults and £5.50 for children.
Tours should be booked in advance by calling
0141 551 4308.

Did You Know?
With a capacity of 60,832, Celtic Park is the largest
football league ground in Scotland and the second
largest in Britain.

Dundee United

Tannadice Park

Ground Name: Tannadice Park
Capacity: 14,209 (all seated)
Address: Tannadice St,
Dundee, DD3 7JW
Telephone No: 01382-833-166
Fax No: 01382-889-398
Pitch Size: 110 x 72 yards
Year Ground Opened: 1909*
Undersoil Heating: Yes
Club Nickname: The Terrors
Home Kit Colours: Tangerine & Black

Official Web Site:
www.dundeeunitedfc.co.uk

Unofficial Website:
Dundee United Mad (Footy Mad Network) –
www.dundeeunited-mad.co.uk

■ What's The Ground Like?

The ground was improved in the 1990's with the construction of two new stands and an extension to the existing Main Stand. One of these is the impressive two-tiered George Fox Stand, running along one side of the pitch. This stand has a large lower tier and a smaller top tier. It opened in 1992 and was named after a former Chairman of the Club. On the other side is the Main (South) Stand, which was renamed the Jerry Kerr Stand in 2003, after a former player and manager. As Aidan Hegarty informs me; 'The original Main Stand was opened in 1962 and holds a place in the history of Scottish football grounds in being the first in Scotland to be constructed with a cantilever roof to provide column free viewing'. It is also unusual in that the stand is slightly 'L'-shaped, just extending around the South East corner of the stadium. Niall Wallace adds; 'It was intended at the time that the whole ground would be rebuilt in a similar manner to the Main Stand, but due to lack of finance it never happened. It is worth noting though that the Club was the first ever to have a glass-fronted lounge in the Main Stand for the benefit of sponsors. This was opened in 1971 and overlooked the pitch, something that is now a common sight in grounds across the country today'.

The Main Stand was extended in 1997 so that it now runs the full length of the pitch. The extension replaced what was known as the 'Fair Play Enclosure', so named as it was funded from an award made to the Club from UEFA in 1987. The stand is two-tiered and has a strip of perspex running across the back of it, just below the roof to allow more light to reach the pitch. The relatively new extension to the stand can be identified as it has an unusual roof jutting out towards the pitch. At one end of the ground is the West Stand (known affectionately as 'The Shed'), a former terrace with seating now fitted to it. Parts of the original terrace that are no longer used for spectators can be seen on either side of it. There are a couple of supporting pillars in this stand that could hinder your view of the pitch. Opposite is the covered two-tiered East Stand, opened in 1994.

What Is It Like For Visiting Supporters?

Away fans are normally housed on one side of the Jerry Kerr (Main) Stand at one side of the pitch, where around 1,000 supporters can be accommodated. For old firm games and local derbies, then the whole of this stand plus the West Stand can also be given to the away support, increasing the allocation to around 5,400. George Hobb, a visiting Hearts supporter adds; 'the ground can sometimes lack a little atmosphere. Plus try to avoid arriving at the ground early, so that you get to miss that awful club mascot!'. I have also received reports of fans being ejected from the ground for persistently standing during the game, so be on your best behaviour.

Where To Drink?

The Centenary bar near to the ground welcomes both home and away supporters. The bar has two rooms within it, one of which is used for home fans and one for away supporters. George Hobb recommends 'The Clep Bar on Clepington Road. Great pies, friendly bar staff and very reasonable prices. It is only five minutes walk from the ground'.

How To Get There & Where To Park?

From The South:
Follow the A90 through Dundee. Leave the A90 at the junction with the B960 (sign posted 'Football Traffic'/Dundee), and turn right onto Clepington Road (B960). Continue along Clepington Road for one mile where you will reach a roundabout. Go straight across the roundabout and after a short distance you should be able to see some floodlights over beyond the houses on your right. Take the 2nd right into Arklay Street and then right into Tannadice Steet for the ground. Street parking.

From The North:
Follow the A90 through Dundee. Leave the A90 at the junction with the B960 (sign posted 'Football Traffic'/Dundee), and turn left onto Clepington Road (B960). Then as directions above.

By Train

Dundee train station is over two miles away from the ground and is quite a walk away from the ground (25-30mins). Best to jump in a taxi.
   Leave the station via the long covered footbridge, take the exit to the right before the walkway enters the Nethergate centre, this exit has steps down to Union Street. Go to the top of Union St & turn right into the High St, after a couple of hundred yards veer left into the pedestrianised Murraygate and proceed to the Wellgate centre. Go via the escalators in the Wellgate centre to the top floor of the centre and exit onto Victoria Road. (If Wellgate is closed, turn left along Panmure Street, right up Meadowside and right onto Victoria Road to rear of Wellgate Shopping Centre).
   Here you have two choices, via the Hilltown (Shorter distance but like climbing the north face of the Eiger) or via Dens Road (much longer but far less likely to induce a heart attack).
   Option 1 (for those fit enough) cross Victoria Road to the foot of the Hilltown walk up this for approx 1/3 mile (it feels like 3) till you reach the junction of Main St & Strathmartine Road this is easily recognisable by the ornamental clock near the junction. Turn right onto Main St and proceed until you reach the junction with Isla St (Church on the corner opposite the excellent Snug Bar). Turn left into Isla St & you will see the ground directly ahead of you.
   Option 2 Turn right onto Victoria Road proceed about 1/4 mile, veer left at the Eagle Mills into Dens Road. Pass Dura Street, Alexander Street and Dens Road Market then right into Arklay Street. Once you reach Tannadice Street you can see the Tannadice ground.
   Neil Gellatly adds; 'Alternatively frequent bus services are available from Albert Square'.
   Thanks to Aidan Hegarty and Neil Gellaty for providing the directions.

Local Rivals

Dundee.

Admission Prices

Like a number of Clubs, Dundee United operate a category system (A & B), whereby the more popular games (Rangers, Celtic, Aberdeen, Hibernian and Hearts + possible cup matches) cost more to watch than others. Prices are below with category B prices shown in brackets.

Home Supporters:

Gordon Fox Stand (Upper Centre):
Adults £27 (£23),
Concessions £15 (£12)

Gordon Fox Stand (Upper Wings):
Adults £25 (£21),
Concessions £13 (£11)

Gordon Fox Stand (Lower Tier):
Adults £22 (£19),
Concessions £11 (£9)

East Stand (Upper Tier):
Adults £25 (£21),
Concessions £13 (£11)

East Stand (Lower Tier):
Adults £22 (£19),
Concessions £12 (£9)

Away Supporters:

Jerry Kerr Stand (Upper Tier):
Adults £25 (£21),
Concessions £12 (£11)

Jerry Kerr Stand (Lower Tier):
Adults £22 (£19),
Concessions £12 (£9)

Concessions apply to under 18's and over 60's.

■ **Programme**
Official Programme £2.

■ **Record Attendance**
28,000 v Barcelona, 1966,
Inter Cities Fairs Cup Competition.

■ **Average Attendance**
2005-2006: 8,198 (Premier League)

■ **Did You Know?**
That the grounds of Dundee United and their rivals
Dundee, are literally only a few hundred yards
apart on the same road. I believe that these two
league grounds are the closest together of any in
Britain.

* Although the ground was officially opened as
Tannadice Park, by the newly formed Dundee
Hibernian Club in 1909, football had been
played at the ground which was originally
called Clepington Park, for some 20 years
prior to this date.

Dunfermline

East End Park

Ground Name: East End Park
Capacity: 11,998 (all seated)
Address: Halbeath Rd,
Dunfermline,
Fife, KY12 7RB
Telephone No: 01383-724-295
Fax No: 01383-723-468
Ticket Office: 0870-300-1201
Ticket Office Fax: 01383-626-452
Pitch Size: 115 x 71 Yards
Year Ground Opened: 1885
Undersoil Heating: Yes
Club Nickname: The Pars
Home Kit Colours: White With Black Stripes

Official Web Site:
www.dafc.co.uk

Unofficial Website:
DAFC.NET - www.dafc.net

■ What's The Ground Like?
The overall look of the ground has greatly improved with the redevelopment of both ends of the ground. The Norrie McCathie & East Stands at each end of the ground, are very similar in design and were opened in 1998. Both are covered single-tiered stands, that are quite steep in appearance. On one side of the ground is the two-tiered South (Main) Stand, which is a classic-looking football stand built in the early 1960s and is of a good size. On the other side is the smaller North Stand, which is single-tiered and covered.

After the Club accepted a grant from UEFA to replace their grass surface with a new experimental artificial pitch, which was installed for the 2003/04 season, the Club have now reverted back to grass at the request of other SPL members. Reaction to the artificial pitch experiment were mixed, especially when visiting sides lost on it!

■ What Is It Like For Visiting Supporters?
Away fans are normally housed in the East Stand at one end of the ground, where just over 3,000 fans can be accommodated. The facilities in this stand are good and the view of the playing action excellent. If demand requires it, then parts of the North & South (Main) Stand can also be allocated for a total of 6,783, which is the allocation for Old Firm games. Other visitors get a maximum of 4,400 seats. There is normally a good atmosphere generated within the ground.

One point of interest is that the winner of the half time lottery is presented with the relevant amount of cash on the pitch. Let's just hope that they don't get mugged on the way home!

■ Where To Drink?
Jim Francis recommends the Elizabethan for away supporters to drink in. Otherwise the ground is around 10-15 minutes walk away from the town centre where there are plenty of pubs to be found.

Dunfermline

■ **How To Get There & Where To Park?**

From North & South :
Leave the M90 at Junction 3. Take the A907 towards Dunfermline. Just keep going straight on this road and you will eventually come to the ground on your right.

From West :
From the A985 take the A994 towards Dunfermline. Keep straight on this road into Dunfermline and you will come to the ground on your left.

■ **Parking**
There is an official car park at the ground (£1) behind the East Stand. Otherwise street parking.

■ **By Train**
There are two stations that are each about a 15-minute walk away from the ground, or about £4 in a taxi. These are Dunfermline Queen Margaret & Dunfermline Town. Both are served by trains from Edinburgh and the latter as the name suggests is closer to the town centre.

■ **Local Rivals**
Falkirk.

■ **Admission Prices**
Like a number of other clubs, admission prices are varied, dependant on the category of opposition.

The categories are A: Rangers, Celtic, Aberdeen, Hearts and Hibernian and B: Other Games.

Home Fans:
Category B prices are shown bracketed

Main Stand:
Adults £24 (£22),
Concessions £16 (£15)
Under 12's £11 (£11)

Other Areas:
Adults* £22 (£21),
Concessions £16 (£13)
Under 12's £11 (£4)
*A discount of £2 is available on these adult prices to fans who are also club members.

Away Fans:

Adults £23 (£21)
Concessions £16 (£13)
Under 12's £11 (£4)

Concessions apply to OAP's, Under 16's and the disabled. Unemployed and students can also qualify for the concessionary rate. This offer applies to home supporters only and proof of status is required.

Dunfermline

■ **Programme**
Official Programme £2.50.

■ **Record Attendance**
27,816 v Celtic, 1968.

■ **Average Attendance**
2004-2005: 6,192 (Premier League)

■ **Did You Know?**
One theory as to why the Club is nicknamed the Pars, is that at one time the team played so badly they were labelled as a bunch of paralytics, which was later shortened to Pars.

Falkirk

Falkirk Stadium

Ground Name:	Falkirk Stadium
Capacity:	6,935 (Includes 735 temporary seats)
Address:	Westfield, Falkirk, FK2 9DX
Telephone No:	01324-624-121
Fax No:	01324-612-418
Pitch Size:	110 x 72 yards
Year Ground Opened:	2004
Undersoil Heating:	Yes
Club Nickname:	Bairns
Home Kit Colours:	Navy Blue, White & Red

Official Web Site:
www.falkirkfc.co.uk

Unofficial Websites:
It's Been Chalked Off - www.thebairninholland.com
Falkirk Mad (Footy Mad Network) –
www.falkirk-mad.co.uk

■ What's The Ground Like?

After leaving their old Brockville Ground in 2003, home since 1876, and then ground sharing with Stenhousemuir for one season, the Club have now taken up residence on the very outskirts of Falkirk.

Opened in July 2004, the Falkirk Stadium as it was named, originally comprised just one stand, but a second smaller stand has since opened in March 2005. The West Stand at one side of the pitch is a huge cantilever affair that houses 4,200 supporters. It looks spectacular both close up and from a distance. In terms of design it is probably one of the best new stands constructed in Britain

for some years. It is two-tiered, with a large lower tier and a small upper tier with comparatively small windshields to either side. At one end is the North Stand. This latest addition to the stadium is a covered all seated stand that has a capacity of 2,000. For this season the Club have also opened a small temporary covered stand at the South end of the stadium, which houses 735 seated fans. The East side of the stadium is currently unused for supporters.

Kevin Dunn adds; 'The Brockville Ground has been demolished and been replaced with a Morrisons superstore. Morrisons have not forgotten the history of the location, and have some rather impressive stained windows with views of Falkirk FC's past'.

■ Future Ground Developments

Kevin Dunn informs me; 'There are then plans to build a South Stand, which will be virtually identical to the North Stand and then an East Stand, which will house a further 4,200 fans. However, these latter two proposals are dependent on the Club securing the necessary finance. If completed the overall capacity will be 12,800'. The club are seeking planning permission for the 2006/07 season to erect another temporary stand on the east side of the ground which would increase the capacity to 8,000.

■ What Is It Like For Visiting Supporters?

Away fans are housed in the North Stand at one end of the stadium. This end is normally split between home and away fans, but for the bigger games then the whole of the 2,000 capacity is allocated to away supporters. I have yet to visit the

stadium to watch a game, but would expect from such a new stand that the facilities will be good and that you will have a good view of the playing action.

■ Where To Drink?
Being on the outskirts of Falkirk there are few bars or even a handy chippy nearby. Probably best to drink somewhere on the way beforehand or else take the 20-25-minute walk into Falkirk town centre where there are plenty of bars to be found. Kevin Dunn informs me; 'There is a bar called Pennies at the old ice rink, just off the Grangemouth Road. Go up Grangemouth Rd towards the town centre and you will pass the college and the old ice rink (which is now an indoor football centre) on the left hand side. The pub is just down the right hand side of the old ice rink, near to the Saturday market'. Lindsey Coombs adds; 'I would recommend the 'Behind the Wall' bar for a drink before the game. It has won supporters awards in the past and is located in the centre of Falkirk, close to Grahamston station.

■ How To Get There & Where To Park?

From The East:
Leave the M9 at Junction 5 and take the A9 towards Falkirk. After about a mile you will be able to see the stadium over on your right.

From The West:
Leave the M9 at Junction 6 and take the A904 towards Falkirk. You will reach the stadium on your left.

The car park at the stadium is for permit holders only. There is another provided for away fans as

Stuart Laing informs me: 'The away fans' car park costs £2 to park in, its entrance is on the Grangemouth Road'. Alternatively there is another car park available at Falkirk College which is a short distance along the A904 towards Falkirk. Otherwise street parking.

■ By Train
Falkirk Grahamston Station is about a mile away from the stadium. It is a fairly straight 20-minute walk down the A904 Grangemouth Road. As you come out of the station turn left and follow the ring road round (A803) to the right. Turn left into Weir Street and at the bottom of the street turn left onto Kerse Lane. This is the A904 which leads into Ladysmill and then becomes Grangemouth Road. Go straight down this road and you will eventually reach the stadium over on your right.

Otherwise any buses that are Grangemouth bound going from Falkirk should also pass the stadium.

■ Local Rivals
St Johnstone & Dunfermline.

■ Admission Prices

Home Fans:

West Stand (Centre):
Adults £20,
no concessions.

West Stand (Wings):
Adults £18,
Concessions £12,
Children Of Primary School Age £10.

North Stand:
Adults £18,
Concessions £12,
Children Of Primary School Age £10.

South (Temporary Stand):
Adults £12,
Concessions £8,
Children Of Primary School Age £4.

Away Fans:

North Stand:
Adults £18,
Concessions £12.

■ Programme
Official Programme £2.

■ Record Attendance
At The Falkirk Stadium:
6,500 v Rangers,
Premier League, September 10th, 2005.

At Brockville:
23,100 v Celtic, February 21st, 1953.

■ Average Attendance
2005-2006: 5,516 (Premier League)

■ Did You Know?
The Club's nickname "Bairns" comes from the
motto of the old Burgh of Falkirk - 'Better meddle
wi' the deil than the Bairns O' Falkirk'.

Heart of Midlothian

Tynecastle Stadium

Ground Name: Tynecastle Stadium
Capacity: 18,008 (all seated)
Address: Gorgie Rd,
Edinburgh, EH11 2NL
Telephone No: 0870-787-1874
Fax No: 0131-200-7222
Pitch Size: 107 x 74 yards
Year Ground Opened: 1886
Undersoil Heating: Yes
Club Nickname: Hearts or Jam Tarts
Home Kit Colours: Maroon & White

Official Web Site:
www.heartsfc.co.uk

Unofficial Websites:
JamboFever - www.jambofever.co.uk
London Hearts - www.londonhearts.com
Planet Hearts - www.planethearts.co.uk
No Idle Talk –
www.zinescene.pwp.blueyonder.co.uk/mynithomepage.htm

■ What's The Ground Like?
The ground has improved greatly with the
redevelopment of three sides of the ground during
the 1990's. The Roseburn, Gorgie & Wheatfield
Stands, are all good sized single-tiered stands, that
are similar in design and height. Only the Main
Stand on one side of the pitch, remains of the

'old Tynecastle. Originally completed just after the
First World War, it looks somewhat out of place
amongst its shiny new neighbours. It is two-tiered,
smaller than the other stands and has a fair few
supporting pillars. On top of this stand perches a
model of an owl, which is there to help deter the
presence of other birds to the ground.

■ What Is It Like For Visiting Supporters?
Away fans are housed in the Roseburn Stand at
one end of the ground, where up to 3,676
supporters can be accommodated. Clubs with a
small following may find that a smaller portion of
this stand is allocated. The steep slope of the stand
ensures a good view of the pitch and the facilities
on offer are good. Apart from the Old Firm games
and local derbies against Hibs, the atmosphere can
be lacking.

■ Where To Drink?
George Hobb informs me; 'The Station Bar in
Gorgie Road to the west of the stadium always
has a warm welcome for away fans. Ryries and
The Haymarket are good pubs and are within
10 minutes walking distance of the ground'.
    George continues; 'Any neutral visitors should of
course visit the legendary Athletic Arms (see
below). Other notable bars include the Tynecastle
Arms, which is only a corner kick away from the
ground and among the memorabilia on display is
the Jersey worn by Super Wayne Foster when he

scored the winning goal Against Hibs in a cup tie a few years ago. For some more football Memorabilia John Robertson's bar is also worth a visit. Both these bars are located In Gorgie Road and get very busy on match days, so get there early'.

My favourite pub near to the ground is the Athletic Arms. The pub, nicknamed 'Diggers' as it overlooks a graveyard, serves great beer and has great service. In fact it not unusual to see fans just ordering with their fingers, as when you just indicate, two, three, four, the barman knows that you just want their excellent ale.

■ How To Get There & Where To Park?
Follow the M8 towards Edinburgh. At the end of the M8 take the A720 (Edinburgh By Pass) southwards towards Dalkeith. Leave the A720 at the junction with the A71 and follow the A71 into Edinburgh. You will eventually reach the ground on your right. Street parking.

■ By Train
The nearest train station is Edinburgh Haymarket, which is a around a 15-minute walk away from the ground. You can see the ground as you come into the station. On leaving the station turn right at the Ryries pub, into Dalry Road. Dalry Road runs into Gorgie Road. About one mile on and the ground is visible from the first major road junction/set of traffic lights.

■ Local Rivals
Hibernian, Rangers & Celtic.

■ Admission Prices
The club operate a category system for matches (A & B), so that admission prices are varied dependant on which club is being played. Category B match prices are shown in brackets:

Home Fans:

Wheatfield Stand (Upper Centre Block D):
Adults £35 (£25),
No Concessions £25 (£15)

Wheatfield Stand (Upper Centre Wings):
Adults £30 (£20),
No Concessions £20 (£10)

Wheatfield Stand (Outer Wings & Lower Tier):
Adults £25 (£15),
Concessions £15 (£5)

Main Stand (Upper Centre):
Adults £25 (£15),
Concessions £15 (£5)

Gorgie Stand (Upper Family Area):
Adults £25 (£15),
Concessions £15 (£5)

All other areas of the ground:
Adults £20 (£10),
Concessions £10 (£5)

Away Fans:

Roseburn Stand (Upper):
Adults £25 (£15),
Concessions £15 (£5)

Roseburn Stand (Lower):
Adults £20 (£10),
Concessions £10 (£5)

Category A games: Celtic, Rangers & Hibernian.

■ Programme & Fanzines
Official Programme £2.50
No Idle Talk Fanzine £1.
ATB (Always the Bridesmaid) Fanzine £1.

■ Record Attendance
53,396 v Glasgow Rangers,
February 13th, 1932.
Scottish Cup 3rd Round.

■ Average Attendance
2005-2006: 16,767 (Premier League)

■ Did You Know?
That the Club got its name from a local dance hall
frequented by the founders of the Club.

Ground Name:	Easter Road
Capacity:	17,500 (all seated)
Address:	12 Albion Place,
	Edinburgh, EH7 5QG
Telephone No:	0131-661-2159
Fax No:	0131-659-6488
Ticket Office:	0131-661-1875
Pitch Size:	112 x 74 yards
Year Ground Opened:	1893
Undersoil Heating:	Yes
Club Nickname:	The Hibees
Home Kit Colours:	Green & White

Official Web Site:
www.hibs.org.uk

Unofficial Websites:
Mass Hibsteria - www.masshibsteria.com/home/index.php
Hibs Net (Rivals Network) - www.hibsforum.co.uk

■ What's The Ground Like?

The ground has improved dramatically with three new stands being built at Easter Road over recent years. The latest addition is the new West Stand which was opened at the beginning of the 2001-2002 season. This is a particularly impressive two-tiered stand, which is now the largest stand at the ground. Its upper tier is much steeper than the lower, with a gap between housing corporate hospitality facilities. This stand is located at one side of the pitch, is unusual in having a large perspex strip in the upper tier, just below the roof, that allows more light into the ground. Both ends are relatively new and virtually identical to one another. Each are two-tiered and look unusual as a small corner of the top tier slopes away at an angle rather than being the normal rectangular shape. The East Stand at one side of the pitch, is a former terrace that has now been made all seated. This is the last of the older stands to remain at the ground and has a fair few supporting pillars. It also has a number of floodlight pylons protruding from its roof.

■ What Is It Like For Visiting Supporters?

Away fans are normally housed in the lower tier of the South Stand at one end. However if demand requires it then the whole of the South Stand can be given to away supporters. Usually a good day out, that is both enjoyable and hassle free.

Peter Llewellyn adds 'On my last visit in May I was reminded of how near Easter Road is to the sea. It was a hot day when I set out and most fans were wearing just a shirt. A sea mist came down during the first half and obscured the top of Arthur's Seat which can be seen clearly in one of

he corners. By the second half mists were swirling
ound the ground and Arthur's Seat had
disappeared. The temperature went from about
25C to about 6 or 7C and it was freezing. I didn't
get completely warm until stopping for a bite to
eat at Biggar on the way home!'

Where To Drink?

im Adie, informs me; 'There are numerous pubs
on Easter Road itself most of which are pretty
friendly for away fans other than Aberdeen.
The Four in Hand and Middletons are particularly
recommended'. Ian McKenzie adds; 'away fans
apart from the local rival clubs) should also be
okay in the Cabbage N Ribs, also on Easter Road'.

How To Get There & Where To Park?

Not the easiest of grounds to find as it is located in
the North East part of Edinburgh, the other side of
the city centre to the way that most people
approach the city from the M8.

From The M8:

At the end of the M8, follow signs for the City
Centre. Upon reaching the City Centre follow signs
or Leith (A900). Continue towards Leith on the
A900 and at the junction with the B1350 turn
ight onto London Road (B1350). It is the fourth
left at the crossroads, onto Easter Road and then

the fourth right into Albion Road for the ground.

From The South: (and avoiding the City Centre)
Follow the A1 into Edinburgh. Turn right onto the
B1350 London Road and then right at the
crossroads into Easter Road. Take the fourth right
into Albion Road for the ground.

By Train

The ground is around a 20-minute walk from
Edinburgh Waverley station. Exit the station via
the Waverley Steps on to Prince's Street. Cross the
road and head for Leith Walk which is about 200
yards diagonally opposite from the exit to the
station. Go straight down Leith Walk for about a
quarter mile and turn right along London Road.
Walk a further half mile to the top of Easter Road
on your left. The Stadium is about 300 yards down
Easter Road on your right hand side. Thanks to Jim
Adie for providing the train station information.

Local Rivals

Heart Of Midlothian.

Admission Prices

Admission prices vary in accordance with the
category of the match. Category A prices are
shown here with category B prices in brackets.

Home Fans:

West Stand Centre:
Adults £25 (£22),
Concessions £10 (£10)

West Stand Upper Wings:
Adults £22 (£20),
Concessions £10 (£10)

West Stand Lower Centre:
Adults £25 (£22),
Concessions £10 (£10)

West Stand Lower Wings:
Adults £22 (£20),
Concessions £10 (£10)

East Stand:
Adults £20 (£18),
Concessions £10 (£10)

Famous Five Stand Upper:
Adults £24 (£20),
 Concessions £10 (£10)

Famous Five Stand Lower:
Adults £22 (£19),
Concessions £10 (£10)

Whyte & Mackay South Stand Upper:
Adults £24 (£20),
Concessions £10 (£10)

Away Fans

Whyte & Mackay South Stand Lower:
Adults £24 (£20),
Concessions £10 (£10).

▨ Programme & Fanzines
Official Programme £2.
Mass Hibsteria Fanzine £1.

▨ Record Attendance
65,860 v Heart Of Midlothian, 1950.

▨ Average Attendance
2005-2006: 13,567 (Premier League)

▨ Did You Know?
That Hibernia was the Roman name for Ireland
and maintains a link with the Irish-born founders
of the Club.

Inverness Caledonian Thistle

Tulloch Caledonian Stadium

Ground Name:	Tulloch Caledonian Stadium
Capacity:	7,500 (all seated)
Address:	East Longman, Inverness, IV1 1FF
Telephone No:	01463-222-880
Fax No:	01463-715-816
Pitch Size:	115 x 75 yards
Year Ground Opened:	1996
Undersoil Heating:	Yes
Club Nickname:	Caley Thistle
Home Kit Colours:	Royal Blue, Red

Official Web Site:
Caley Thistle Online - http://hmssneck.co./official/

Unofficial Websites:
Caley Nostalgia - www.caledonianfc.co.uk
Write On Caley - http://writeoncaley.tripod.com
Caley Jags - www.caleyjags.com

■ What's The Ground Like?
With the SPL reducing its stadium capacity requirements, the Club have at last been able to develop the stadium. Mainly to fulfil the criteria, the club have built two new stands at either end of the ground and installed undersoil heating. Not only has this meant that the Club have not had to seek an alternative site to build a bigger stadium, but also that the ground-sharing agreement with the Club at Aberdeen has now ended and the Club have been able to return home.

The ground is dominated by the Main Stand, which runs along one side of the pitch. This all seated stand is quite smart looking and is partly covered (to the rear), whilst opposite is a small open terrace, that is now unused. At one end is the North Stand or more commonly known as the 'Bridge End', which is an all seated covered stand which is the 'home end' of the ground. The other end, the South Stand, is a similar-looking all seated stand, that is given to away supporters.
One unusual fact about the Caledonian Stadium is that it has the widest pitch of any league team in Scotland.

The Club was formed in 1994, following a merger of two Clubs; Inverness Thistle & Caledonian FC. The new Club were admitted to the Scottish League for the 1994-95 season.

■ What Is It Like For Visiting Supporters?
Away supporters are housed in the new South Stand at one end of the ground, where up to 2,200 fans can be accommodated. John Hill informs me; 'The ground is very smart and there's a great atmosphere when it's a full house. The ground staff are also very welcoming and the location is pretty good, with some stunning views over the water. The only real let down, was the lack of a supporters club at the ground or any nearby pubs. Otherwise, the catering almost makes up for the lack of beer, especially the brilliant steak sandwiches!'

The ground is built right on the coast of the Moray Firth, means that there can be some biting cold winds coming off the sea. However, the ground has quite a picturesque setting and from the away end you get quite a view of the Kessock Bridge climbing up into the distance.

■ Where To Drink?
John Blair informs me; 'There are no pubs as yet around the ground. There is due to be one opened at the ground, but at the moment the nearest pubs

Inverness Caledonian Thistle

are about half a mile away towards town centre. In town there are plenty of good pubs. Try the Gellions, the Phoenix or Gunsmiths, or the Caley Club (near Caledonian FC's old ground) which has plenty of history. Most home fans tend to head for The Innes Bar in Innes Street near the harbour. It's about a 20-minute walk from the stadium'.

■ How To Get There & Where To Park?

From The South:
The ground is straightforward to find and depending on which approach you take into Inverness, the bright orange cantilevers of the Main Stand can be seen for quite some distance away. Continue on the A9 through Inverness and at the roundabout, just before the large bridge across the Moray Firth, turn right for the road down to the ground. There are a couple of good sized car parks (£1) at each end of the ground.

■ By Train

Inverness station, is about a mile away from the ground, which is about a 20-25-minute walk away. On leaving Inverness station follow the signs for the car park and bus station (going along Railway Terrace). Cross through the car park, keeping the bus station on your left and on your right you can see a bridge crossing the River Ness. Go across the bridge and then continue straight ahead along Longman Road. Eventually you will reach the stadium on your left.

Thanks to Ingo Braun for the directions and who also adds; 'After the match there were a number of shuttle buses waiting outside the stadium to take fans back into the town centre'.

■ Local Rivals

Ross County.

■ Admission Prices

Like a number of other clubs admission prices are varied, dependant on the category and opposition. The categoris are A: Rangers and Celtic and B: other games. Category B prices are shown below in brackets.

Home Fans:

    Main Stand:
    Adults £27 (£25),
    Concessions £22 (£20)

    North Stand:
    Adults £22 (£20),
    Concessions £17 (£15)

    North Stand (Family Enclosure):
    Adults £12 (£15),
    Concessions £15 (£13),
    Under 16's £9 (£7)

28 ● A Fan's Guide: Football Grounds – Scotland

way Fans:

South Stand:
Adults £22 (£20),
Concessions £17 (£15)

Programme
fficial Programme £2.50

Record Attendance
t The Caledonian Stadium:
7,512 v Glasgow Rangers,
Premier League, August 6th, 2005.

t Pittodrie (whilst ground sharing with Aberdeen):
9,530 v Aberdeen,
Premier League, October 16th, 2004.

Average Attendance
005-2006: 5,061 (Premier League)

Did You Know?
Vith 26 letters, the Club have the longest name in
cottish & English League football.

Kilmarnock

Rugby Park

Ground Name: Rugby Park
Capacity: 18,128 (all seated)
Address: Rugby Park,
Kilmarnock, KA1 2DP
Telephone No: 01563-545-300
Fax No: 01563-522-181
Ticket Office No: 01563-545-318
Year Ground Opened: 1899
Undersoil Heating: Yes
Pitch Size: 115 x 74 yards
Club Nickname: Killie
Home Kit Colours: Blue, White & Red

Official Web Site:
www.kilmarnockfc.co.uk

Unofficial Websites:
Killie Fever - www.killiefever.co.uk
Kilmarnock Mad (Footy Mad Network) –
www.kilmarnock-mad.co.uk
Killiefc.com - www.killiefc.com

■ What's The Ground Like?

The ground has been transformed with the building of three new stands in the mid 1990's. Both ends of the ground and one side have been redeveloped. The ends are good sized two-tiered stands, which are virtually identical. One of these ends, the Chadwick Stand is given to away supporters. There are also electric scoreboards placed on the roof of each end. The East Stand on one side of the pitch is also a relatively new stand that is similar in height to the two ends. This stand however, does not run the full length of the pitch. Opposite is the older Main Stand, which dates back to the early 1960's. It is smaller than the other stands and has a fair number of supporting pillars which could obstruct your view. The stadium has unusual-looking floodlights protruding from the roofs of the two side stands.

What Is It Like For Visiting Supporters?

Away fans are housed in the Chadwick Stand at one end of the pitch. The facilities and views from this stand are generally very good, although I have had some fans comment that the leg room is a little tight. David Tennant, a visiting St Mirren supporter adds; 'a great ground to visit, with friendly supporters, some good pubs and also don' forget to sample their legendary pies'.

Where To Drink?

Gordon Duff recommends the Howard Arms, in Glencairn Square, which is only a few minutes wall away from the ground. Otherwise, the ground is not that far from the town centre where there are plenty of bars to be found.

How To Get There & Where To Park?

From the A71, take the A759 towards Kilmarnock. Eventually the ground will appear on your left. Turn left off the A735 into South Hamilton Road and le gain into Rugby Road for the ground. The ground quite well signposted around the town. Street arking.

By Train

lmarnock Station is served by trains from lasgow. The ground is around about 15-20 inutes walk away from the station. Emerging om the train station you will find yourself at the p of John Finnie Street. Walk sown this street gainst the flow of one way traffic. At the traffic ghts at the bottom of the street (by the Sheriff ourt) turn right into Portland Road. Take the cond left at the traffic lights into South Hamilton reet and proceed to first right turn into Rugby oad and the ground. Thanks to Stephen Millar for roviding the directions.

Local Rivals

yr United.

Admission Prices

on Old Firm Games:

All areas of the ground:
Adults £18,
Concessions (OAP's/U16's) £12.
Under 16's can gain admission to the
Moffat Stand for £5.

ld Firm Games:

Home Fans:
Adults £22,
Concessions £12

Away Fans:
Adults £22,
No Concessions

Programme

fficial Programme £1.50.

Record Attendance

35.995 v Rangers,
Scottish Cup, March 10th, 1962.

Average Attendance

005-2006: 7,071 (Premier League)

■ Did You Know?

The Club were founded by a group of cricketers who wanted to pursue another sport in the winter to keep fit. They first played rugby for three years before changing to football. Hence the naming of the ground; Rugby Park.

Kilmarnock

Motherwell

Fir Park

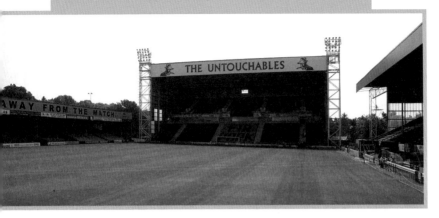

Ground Name: Fir Park
Capacity: 13,742 (all seated)
Address: Fir Park,
Motherwell, ML1 2QN
Telephone No: 01698-333-333
Fax No: 01698-276-333
Ticket Office: 01698-338-002
Pitch Size: 110 x 75 yards
Year Ground Opened: 1895
Undersoil Heating: Yes
Club Nickname: The Well or The Steelmen
Home Kit Colours: Amber & Claret

Official Web Site:
www.motherwellfc.co.uk

Unofficial Websites:
Motherwellfc.org - www.motherwellfc.org
Supporters Trust - www.welltrust.net
Fir Park Corner (Footy Mad Network) –
www.motherwell-mad.co.uk
Welltrustfc.net - www.welltrustfc.net

What's The Ground Like?
The stadium is dominated by the large South Stand at one end. Almost twice the height of the other stands, it is two-tiered with a row of executive boxes running across the middle. Opposite, the Davie Cooper Stand, is a small covered seated stand. The single-tiered Main Stand on one side of the ground, is both raised above pitch level and set back from it. This older stand has windshields to either side as well as a few supporting pillars. It is unusual in that the stand itself doesn't run the full

length of the pitch, but the supporting steelwork does, making for an odd-looking sight. According to Simon Inglis in his book 'The Football Grounds Of Great Britain', this was because it was originally intended in 1962 to build a full length stand but due to a dispute with an owner of a house beyond the corner of that ground (a dispute which the club lost) it was never completed as intended.
This stand was funded chiefly from the sale at that time of Ian St John & Pat Quinn to Liverpool.
This did not go down well with the fans as many subsequently boycotted the stand and to this day it is the most sparsely-populated section of the ground. Opposite is the smaller East Stand, which also has a number of supporting pillars, running across it.

What Is It Like For Visiting Supporters?
Away fans are housed in the South Stand at one end of the pitch. Normally only the lower tier is opened for away fans, but if demand requires it, then the upper tier can be opened also. Up to 5,000 fans can be accommodated in the two tiers. The view of the playing action from this stand is pretty good, as well as the facilities. David Tennant, a visiting St Mirren supporter adds; 'Overall Fir Park is a good day out. The huge away stand was very nice to be in and the atmosphere was alright. No hassle around the ground, but some good banter was had with the home support.'

Where To Drink?
Craig Barry recommends the 'Jack Daniels Bar, which is the closest to the ground. It is popular with both home and away fans, each having their own bar'. Whilst Craig Irving adds; 'The Fir Park

Social Club is on the same road as the ground and is an extremely friendly boozer. Away fans are normally admitted, although restrictions may be put in place for Old Firm games'.

■ How To Get There & Where To Park?
Leave the M74 at Junction 6 and head towards Motherwell. At the first set of lights that you come to turn right onto the B754 (Airbles Road) towards Wishaw. The ground is at the end of this road on the right. Street parking.

■ By Train
Airbles station is the closest to the ground, but is only served by a local service. You are more likely to end up instead at Motherwell Central station, which is around a 15-minute walk away from the ground. Alan McAulay adds; 'You exit the train station facing the main shopping street in the direction of the ground; go straight along it through the shopping precinct/centre; past the shopping centre car park, which leads to an underpass; go under the underpass, up the stairs and turn right; go straight on and the large stand gradually comes into view from behind Wilsons Furniture Store. The road 'forks' at this point with away fans, and those going into the old seated terrace going to the left and all other fans to the right. Away fans walking from Motherwell should note, that the road to the away end is a long and winding one (you think you're there when you see the stand, but it takes about another 5 minutes to access it), so should allow plenty of time. There is also a pretty good pub right next to Motherwell Central, but fans should remember to leave on time; the last time I was in Motherwell I missed the first ten minutes!'

■ Local Rivals
Airdrie United & Hamilton.

■ Admission Prices
Admission prices for home supporters vary dependent on the category of match. The club operate a standard and premium category. Standard prices are shown in brackets:

Main Stand:
Adults £24 (£20),
Concessions £15 (£13),
Juveniles £11 (£9)

East Stand:
Adults £18 (£16),
Concessions £13 (£11),
Juveniles £8 (£6)

Davie Cooper Stand:
Adults £20 (£18),
Concessions £14 (£12),
Juveniles £9 (£7),
Adult + 1 child £25 (£23)

way Fans
Motorola Stand:
Adults £20 (£18),
Concessions £14 (£12),
Juveniles £9 (£7).

Programme
fficial Programme £2.

Record Attendance
35,632 v Glasgow Rangers, 1952.

Average Attendance
005-2006: 6,250 (Premier League)

Did You Know?
he Club are unofficially nicknamed 'The Dossers',
which was attributed by a local paper to the
eague Championship winning side of 1932,
who labelled the laid back passing style of the
eam as 'those Dossers fae the Shire' (Lanarkshire).

Rangers

Ibrox Stadium

Ground Name: Ibrox Stadium
Capacity: 50,411 (all seated)
Address: 150 Edmiston Drive, Glasgow, G51 2XD
Telephone No: 0870-600-1972
Fax No: 0870-600-1978
Ticket Office: 0870-600-1993
Stadium Tours: 0870-600-1972
Pitch Size: 115 x 78 yards
Year Ground Opened: 1899
Undersoil Heating: Yes
Club Nickname: The Gers or Teddy Bears
Home Kit Colours: Blue, Red & White

Official Web Site:
www.rangers.co.uk

Unofficial Websites:
Follow, Follow (Footy Mad Network) –
www.followfollow.com
Supporters Trust - www.rangerssupporterstrust.co.uk
The Blue Order - www.theblueorder.co.uk
Blue Nose Bars - www.bluenosebars.com

■ What's The Ground Like?
The ground was mostly redeveloped in the late 1970's and early 1980's with three new stands being constructed. Only the Main Stand (which was originally built in 1929) at one side of the pitch remains of the old Ibrox. This stand has also been refurbished and in 1994 a third tier was added to it. The impressive red brick facade of this stand was left intact (it is a listed building), which means that the ground has a great blend of modern facilities, whilst still retaining its historic character. The three relatively new stands are all good sized two-tiered stands and either side of the Govan Stand, the corners have been filled, with seating in the lower tier and large video screens in the upper tier. Even though the Main Stand is larger than the other stands, the ground looks well balanced as the roof of this stand comes down to the same height of the others. The corners to either side of this stand are partly open, being filled with stairwells. There are also a couple of small electric scoreboards at either end of the ground. Overall a superb ground that is arguably one of the best in Britain.

■ Future Ground Developments
The Club have proposed plans to add a third tier to the Govan Stand. This would boost the capacity of Ibrox to around 58,000. However as of yet no firm timescales have been announced for this development to take place.

What Is It Like For Visiting Supporters?

Away fans are located in the lower tier of the Broomloan Stand, towards the Govan Stand and the bulk are located in this corner of the ground, below one of the large video screens. The facilities are fairly good in this area, as well as enjoying a decent view of the playing action. For big games such as the Old Firm derby, then the whole of the Broomloan Stand can be allocated to the away support. Although the ground itself is great, I found Ibrox to be quite intimidating. I would advise that you exercise caution around the ground and to keep club colours covered.

Although most games sell out at Ibrox, tickets can be bought for most games, as long as you call the ticket office at least a couple of weeks prior to the fixture.

Where To Drink?

Most bars around the vicinity of the ground are normally very crowded and not particularly away fan friendly, so it may as well be an idea to drink in the city centre before moving onto the ground. However, The Albion on Broomloan Road by the ground, has been recommended by some away fans.

James Prentice adds; 'Away supporters tend to head for bars towards the Centre of Glasgow, as there is less chance of any hassle than when around the ground. For Rangers fans, there are several good bars to be found around Ibrox. There is the District Bar on Paisley Road West, which is an excellent, typical Glaswegian pub, and the Louden Bar, which is just around the corner - a Rangers fan's heaven and a real Rangers pub. The Stadium Bar on Copland Road is OK. There are also chip shops and a plethora of chip and burger vans around the ground of matchdays, as would be expected. Also, there is a relatively new café in a car park opposite Ladbrokes' Bookmakers on Copland Road which serves good meals at cheap prices'.

How To Get There & Where To Park?

Leave the M8 at Junction 23 and head towards Govan/Clyde Tunnel on the A8 Paisley Road West. You will come to the stadium on your right after about a mile and a half. The roads around Ibrox become pretty congested, so please allow some extra time for your journey. Street parking.

By Train/Underground

The ground is at least a couple of miles away from Glasgow Central & Queens Street railway stations. Either jump in a taxi, or proceed down Argyll Street to the St Enoch Underground Station and take the

Rangers

Inner Circle underground train to the ground. Ibrox has its own underground station, only a few minutes walk away. The station, however, gets exceptionally busy after the games. Alternatively, there always seems to be a number of buses running by the ground which are heading back into the City Centre.

James Prentice adds; 'Ibrox Underground has huge queues after games, and some supporters may prefer to use Cessnock Underground Station on Paisley Road West, as fewer people seem to use it on a matchday. Turn out of the stadium and go left on to Edminston Drive, and the station is about five minutes' walk away after the road joins up with Paisley Road West (Adult single tickets are about 80p). While it is a tiny bit longer to walk to Cessnock, you may well stand a better chance of getting on the Underground more quickly than at Ibrox. Buses also run along Paisley Road West, and can take you right into the City Centre every couple of minutes. Getting off at Bridge Street is about 90p Single and is a two-minute walk over the River Clyde for the Centre of Glasgow'. Otherwise if you are feeling particularly brave you can embark on the 40-minute walk back to the city centre.

■ **Local Rivals**
Celtic.

■ **Admission Prices**

Home Fans:

Main Stand Club Deck:
Adults £23

Main Stand:
Adults £23

Govan Stand (Upper Tier):
Adults: £23

Govan Stand (Lower Tier):
Adults £22

Broomloan Stand:
Adults £22

Copland Stand:
Adults £22

Under 18's (all areas): £12
Over 65's (all areas) £12

Away Fans:

Govan West Corner:
Adults £22,
Concessions £12.

■ **Programme & Fanzine**
Official Programme £2.
Fanzine: Follow, Follow £1.50.

■ **Record Attendance**
118,567 v Celtic 1939.

■ **Average Attendance**
2005-2006: 49,245 (Premier League)

■ **Stadium Tours**
The Club normally offer tours of the ground on Thursdays, Fridays & Sundays. In the school holidays these are offered daily from Monday to Friday. The tour lasts around 90 minutes and costs £7 for adults and £5 concessions. Tours can be booked by calling 0870 600 1972.

■ **Did You Know?**
That ground name of Ibrox was taken from the name of a district in Glasgow.

St Mirren

St Mirren Park

Ground Name: St Mirren Park,
but many fans still like
to call it Love Street.
Capacity: 10,800 (all seated)
Address: Love St, Paisley,
Renfrewshire, PA3 2EJ
Telephone No: 0141-889-2558
Fax No: 0141-848-6444
Ticket Office: 0141-840-4100
Ticket Office Fax: 0141-848-9222
Pitch Size: 110 x 70 yards
Year Ground Opened: 1895
Club Nickname: The Buddies
Home Kit Colours: Black & White

Official Web Site:
www.stmirren.net

Unofficial Websites:
Black And White Army - www.blackandwhitearmy.com
St Mirren Info - www.stmirren.info
Independent Supporters Association –
www.saintsquarterly.co.uk
St Mirren Mad (Footy Mad Network) –
www.stmirren-mad.co.uk

■ What's The Ground Like?

The ground shows both signs of its age and the ambition that is within the club. The Main Stand is a simple top level and enclosure design stretching only halfway along the pitch straddling the halfway line. This stand is the smallest and oldest of the four. Directly opposite the Main Stand is the LDV North Stand. This holds 4,200 fans and is popular with the hardcore St. Mirren fans. It is a seated terrace with shed style roof stretching the length of the pitch. Access to this stand is by means of a large ramp, which stretches from the North East turnstiles over the corner and into the back of the stand. The Away stand is the Laidlaw Scott (West) stand, which is situated at one end of the pitch. This can hold 3,000 away fans but is rarely used completely. The most unusual thing about this stand is that it has a large external staircase on one side, which the away support climb before embarking down the steeply raked stand. This is because the undercroft of the stand is taken up with indoor training pitches. At the other end is the Reid Kerr College Family Stand. This is a 2,200-capacity seated terrace with a cantilevered roof. Thanks to David Tennant for providing a lot of the information on this page.

■ Future Developments

The Club have finally received permission to

change the use of Love Street from a leisure to a retail facility. This will now allow the Club to sell the ground to a supermarket chain, which will help the Club reduce its current level of debt. The Club will move to a new stadium which will be built as a site at Greenhill Road, approximately half a mile west of Love Street. The new stadium would closely resemble Airdrie United's New Broomfield stadium, with 4 separate single-tier stands giving a capacity of around 8,000. Firm timescales have yet to be announced as to when this will take place.

■ What Is It Like For Visiting Supporters?
Away fans are normally located in the West section of the North Stand at one side of the pitch. For big games away fans are given the best seats in the house located in the large Caledonia stand, where up to 3,000 can be accommodated. I have not heard of fans getting hassle outside the ground but caution should be exercised due to the ground location. The ground can be noisy inside and can on occasion make for an intimidating atmosphere.

■ Where To Drink?
There are a couple of pubs near to the ground, although with the close proximity of the town centre many tend to drink there before heading to the game. The Wee Barrel on Love Street itself is a smallish, two-roomed pub which gets very busy

before games, but on my visit there was a good mix of home and away support and the service was good. George Clarke adds; 'The Cottage Arms next to a Chinese takeaway just off Greenock Road has long been a popular haunt for away fans, as the away coaches park up near there on Clark Street and it is only a few minutes walk away from the ground'. In the town centre Peter Balmforth recommends The Argyll Bar and the Hole In the Wa' on Old Sneddon Street, which are both close to a chippy and bookies, although colours should be kept covered. Peter adds 'if you're arriving by train then just outside the station entrance, is a Wetherspoons outlet called the Last Post. However please note that fans are not admitted wearing colours,'.Rene, a visiting Celtic supporter informs me: 'I found the Wallace Bar on Causeyside Street in the town centre to be a friendly enough place to enjoy a beer'.

■ How To Get There & Where To Park?
The ground is particularly easy to get to due to its proximity to the M8. Away fans travelling from the east side of Paisley should make their way to the M8 and continue westbound to junction 29, the St. James interchange. They should then turn left into the Greenock road towards the town centre until they reach Albion Street on the left. From here away fans should be able to enter the Caledonia

tand. Parking is not available at the ground so
eople should park in the surrounding streets.
 would personally recommend parking nearer to
 he town centre in one of the car parks. Car parks
 an be found off Moss Street, and some places can
 e found behind the court in Glen Street. Failing
 his, Glasgow Airport is only around half a mile
 rom the ground (though it can be expensive).

By Train
 aisley Gilmour Street is on a main line from
 ilasgow Central Station and is only 400 yards
 rom the ground. As you come out of the station
 ntrance walk up the road straight in front of you
 ind turn right at the Last Post pub and then right
 igain so that you are coming back on yourself
 (the ground is effectively behind the station).
 io straight down this road going under a railway
 iridge and at the crossroads with the busy A726
 jo straight on which brings you into Love Street.
 The ground is down this road on the left.

Local Rivals
 ireenock Morton.

Admission Prices

Home Fans:

Main Stand & Enclosure
Adults £15,
Concessions £8.

LDV North Stand
Adults £13,
Concessions £7,
1 Adult + 1 Child £17,
Each additional child £4.

Reid Kerr College (East) **Stand**
Adults £13,
Concessions £7,
1 Adult + 1 Child £17,
Each additional child £4.

Away Fans:

Laidlaw Scott (West) **Stand**
Adults £15,
Concessions £8,
1 Adult + 1 Child £20,
Each additional child £4.

Programme
Official Programme £2.

Record Attendance
47,438 v Celtic, August 20th 1949.

Average Attendance
2005-2006: 3,798 (Division One)

Did You Know?
The Club is named after St Mirren, the Patron Saint
of Paisley.

Airdrie United

Excelsior Stadium

Ground Name: Excelsior Stadium (although most Airdrie fans call it New Broomfield)
Capacity: 10,171 (all seated)
Club Contact Address: 60 St Enoch Square, Glasgow, G1 4AG
Telephone No: 07710-230775
Fax No: 0141-221-1497
Pitch Size: 115 x 75 yards
Year Ground Opened: 1998
Club Nickname: Diamonds
Home Kit Colours: White, Red & Black

Official Web Site:
www.airdrieunitedfc.com

Unofficial Websites:
Broomfield Stomp (Sport Network) – www.sportnetwork.net/main/s2.htm
Ceefax's Airdrie United Website – http://www.geocities.com/ceefax_aufc_1/index.html
Vital Airdrie United (Vital Football Network) – http://www.airdrie.vitalfootball.co.uk/index.asp

■ What's The Ground Like?
The Club was formed in June 2002, after the Airdrieonians Football Club went out of business. The new Airdrie United club was successful in the takeover of another club, Clydebank FC. Airdrie United were subsequently given permission to take Clydebank's place in the league. Unsurprisingly Airdrie United have taken up residence at the same ground that Aidrieonians played at.

The Excelsior Stadium is a smart-looking all seated ground comprising four separate, single-tiered, covered stands. The Jack Dalziel Stand (named after a former Airdrieonians Chairman) at one side of the pitch, is the largest of the four stands. Impressive looking, it has a row of executive boxes running across the back. The other three stands are of an equal height which gives the ground a balanced look. The corners of the ground are open apart from the tall floodlights.

■ What Is It Like For Visiting Supporters?
The modern ground is certainly an excellent one and the facilities available are not bad. However, the atmosphere generated within the ground can be quite lacking at times. For most games the ground is only a quarter full and just a couple of stands (and for some games only one stand) are open. It would be great to return to this ground to see a game in front of a full house, as that would then do it justice.

Away fans are normally located in the East Stand at one side of the pitch. Dependent on away numbers, you may find only the portion of the West Stand allocated (this stand is shared with home supporters) or just the East Stand, or both. In the event that the Club were to draw one of the Old Firm sides, then the Club would give their maximum allocation of away seats (6,500), comprising all the stadium apart from the West Stand.

■ Where To Drink?
There is a supporters bar at the ground, within the Jack Dalziel Stand. Otherwise as John McCleod informs me; 'the nearest pub is the Albert which is a good ten minutes walk away from the ground'.

■ How To Get There & Where To Park?
Leave the M8 at Junction 6, the Newhouse Junction and take the A73 towards Cumbernauld. After two miles turn right into Petersburn Road

38058) and you will see the ground over on the
left. There is a fair sized car park at the ground,
which costs £2. Away fans have their own
entrance to the car park, which is signposted on
approaching the ground. Chris Cobb adds 'allow
extra time for your journey as the access roads
round Airdrie do tend to get quite clogged up'.

By Train

The closest station to the ground is Drumgeloch,
which is around a 5-10-minute walk away. Gary
Sneddon provides these directions to the ground;
Come out of the station and turn right and then
right again, which takes you over the bridge across
the railway. Follow Crowood Drive down the hill
and then right into Bankhead Avenue. Follow this
road around to the left and then taking a right at
the first crossroads into Willow Drive. Follow this
road around to the right until you reach the shops
then take the first left into Craigneuk Avenue.
The ground is at the bottom of this road on the
left-hand side. Please note that Airdrie station is a
good 20-minute walk away from the ground.

Local Rivals

Albion Rovers, Hamilton & Motherwell.

Admission Prices

Adults £15
Concessions £7
1 Adult + 1 Child £20

Programme

Official Programme £2.

Record Attendance

For An Airdrie United Match:
5,709 v Morton
Division Two, May 15th 2004

For The Stadium:
Aidrieonians v Celtic
8,995, League Cup, August 1998

Average Attendance

2005-2006: 1,426 (Division One)

Did You Know?

The stadium gets its name from Excelsior FC, who
were formed in 1878 and later became known as
Airdrieonians.

Clyde

Broadwood Stadium

Ground Name: Broadwood Stadium
Capacity: 8,029 (all seated)
Address: Ardgoil Drive
Cumbernauld, G68 9NE
Telephone No: 01236-451-511
Fax No: 01236-733-490
Pitch Size: 112 x 76 yards
Year Ground Opened: 1995
Club Nickname: Bully Wee
Home Kit Colours: White, Red & Black

Official Web Site:
www.clydefc.co.uk

Unofficial Website:
Clyde Mad (Footy Mad network) –
www.clyde-mad.co.uk

■ What's The Ground Like?
The ground was opened in 1995, after a period of ground sharing with Hamilton & Partick Thistle, following their departure from their old Shawfield ground in 1986. The ground has only three sides, the North End being unused. These stands are single-tiered, have windshields to either side and are all seated and covered affairs. The stands are roughly of the same size and height, although the Main Stand, at one side of the pitch, is slightly taller than the other two. This stand has some enclosed corporate seating at the back.

■ Future Ground Developments
The Club have to plans to build a fourth stand at the North End of the stadium. However there are no firm timescales as to when this will take place and it is probably now only likely if the Club achieve promotion to the Premier League.

■ What Is It Like For Visiting Supporters?
Away supporters are housed in the West Stand at one side of the pitch. The view of the playing action, leg room and the facilities within the stand are both pretty good. The empty North part of the ground gives some pleasant views of the Campsie Hills, but can also allow a biting cold wind to enter the ground, so make sure you wrap up well. In fact some visiting fans have nicknamed the ground 'Ice Station Broadwood'. Still, if you need some central heating then the pies are pretty good. The atmosphere can be a bit flat at times, in an attempt to liven things up, if Clyde score, then 'Dare' by the Gorillaz, blasts out around the ground.

Where To Drink?

onnie Wallace, a visiting Airdrie supporter, informs ne; 'There is a Brewers Fayre pub/restaurant near o the ground off the Craiglinn roundabout. There re other pubs in the neighbouring housing estate f Balloch, however, finding them (or finding your vay back!) in the maze of pedestrian walkways an prove quite challenging'. Otherwise in the earby village of Condorrat there is the Masonic \rms pub. To find this pub from the front of the tadium go up to the roundabout and turn right, hen left at the next roundabout. The pub is just on our left as you enter the village.

How To Get There & Where To Park?

"he ground is situated on the outskirts of :umbernauld, just off the A80 Stirling Road. "he ground is well signposted from the A80 and here is a good sized car park at the ground, vhich costs £2 (it is free though for season ticket olders). However, it can take some time after the jame to get out of it.

By Train

"he nearest station, is Croy station which is about a 20-minute walk away from the ground. "his station is served by trains from Glasgow Queen Street.

Local Rivals

Partick Thistle.

Admission Prices

Adults £14
Over 65's £7
Under 18's £5
Parent + 1 Child £18.

Programme

Official Programme £2.50

Record Attendance

At Broadwood:
8,000 v Celtic
Scottish Cup 3rd Round, January 8th, 2006.

At Shawfield:
52,000 v Rangers
Division I, November 21st, 1908

Average Attendance

2005-2006: 1,285 (Division One)

Did You Know?

That Broadwood is the highest league ground in Scotland (in terms of being above sea level).

Ground Name: Dens Park
Capacity: 12,085 (all seated)
Address: Sandeman St,
Dundee, DD3 7JY
Telephone No: 01382-889-966
Fax No: 01382-832-284
Pitch Size: 101m x 66m
Year Ground Opened: 1899
Undersoil Heating: Yes
Club Nickname: Dark Blues
Home Kit Colours: Dark Blue, Red & White

Official Web Site:
www.dundeefc.co.uk

Unofficial Websites:
Dee-licious - http://dfcdelicious.homestead.com/index.html
Boab's Dundee Site –
http://members.tripod.co.uk/BoabL/index-3.html
Glasgow Dees - www.glasgowdees.tk
Dundee Diehards - www.dundeediehards.tk
Supporters Society - www.dee4life.org.uk

■ What's The Ground Like?
The overall look of the ground has greatly improved with the redevelopment of both ends. The Bobby Cox & Bob Shankly Stands are similar-looking, both being single-tiered and roughly of the same height. Both sides are quite old-looking stands. The Main (North) Stand is a covered seated stand, unusual in that it is oval in shape, meaning that those sitting on the half way line are furthest away from the playing action. In fact at one time the whole ground was oval. It also has only a small amount of seats in the lower portion of the stand, with the bulk of the seating in the upper part. On the other side is a more conventional single-tiered stand, that only runs for about two-thirds of the length of the pitch. Both these stands have many supporting pillars that may hinder your view.

■ What Is It Like For Visiting Supporters?
Away fans are housed in the Bob Shankly Stand at one end of the ground, where up to 3,000 supporters can be accommodated. If required then a further 1,000 seats can be allocated in the Main (North) Stand towards the Bob Shankly End. The facilities within the Bob Shankly Stand are quite good and the view of the playing action excellent. The great thing about this stand is that even a relatively small number of away fans can really generate some noise. George Hobb, a visiting Hearts supporter adds 'normally a relaxed and friendly day out and the atmosphere generated within the ground can be quite good'.

■ Where To Drink?
The Centenary bar near to the ground welcomes

oth home and away supporters. The bar has two ooms within it, one of which is used for home ans and one for away supporters. George Hobb ecommends 'The Clep bar on Clepington Road. Great pies, friendly bar staff and very reasonable prices. It is only five minutes walk from the ground'.

■ How To Get There & Where To Park?

Follow the A90 through Dundee. Leave the A90 at the junction with the B960 (sign posted 'Football Traffic'/Dundee), and turn right onto Clepington Road (B960). Continue along Clepington Road for one mile where you will reach a roundabout. Go straight across the roundabout and after a short distance you should be able to see some floodlights over beyond the houses on your right. Take the 2nd right into Arklay Street and then right into Tannadice Steet. Dens Park is up at the end of this street on the left. There is an official car park behind the Bob Shankly Stand which costs £2 per car, otherwise street parking.

■ By Train

Dundee train station is over two miles away from the ground and is quite a walk away from the ground (25-30mins). Best to jump in a taxi.

Leave the station via the long covered footbridge, take the exit to the right before the walkway enters the Nethergate centre; this exit has steps down to Union Street. Go to the top of Union St & turn right into the High St, after a couple of hundred yards veer left into the pedestrianised Murraygate and proceed to the Wellgate centre. Go via the escalators in the Wellgate centre to the top floor of the centre and exit onto Victoria Road. (If Wellgate is closed, turn left along Panmure Street, right up Meadowside and right onto Victoria Road to rear of Wellgate Shopping Centre).

Here you have two choices, via the Hilltown (Shorter distance but like climbing the north face of the Eiger) or via Dens Road (much longer but far less likely to induce a heart attack).

Option 1 (for those fit enough); cross Victoria Road to the foot of the Hilltown walk up this for approx 1/3 mile (it feels like 3) till you reach the junction of Main St & Strathmartine Road this is easily recognisable by the ornamental clock near the junction. Turn right onto Main St and proceed until you reach the junction with Isla St (Church on the corner opposite the excellent Snug Bar). Turn left into Isla Street (at Clepington Church). Continue across Dens Road into North Isla Street

and turn left at Tannadice. Dens Park is just up the road.

Option 2; Turn right onto Victoria Road proceed about 1/4 mile, veer left at the Eagle Mills into Dens Road. Pass Dura Street, Alexander Street and Dens Road Market then right into Arklay Street. Once you reach Tannadice Street turn left past Tannadice, Dens Park is just up the road.

Neil Gellatly adds; 'Alternatively frequent bus services are available from Albert Square.

Thanks to Neil Gellatly for providing the directions.

■ Local Rivals
Dundee United.

■ Admission Prices

All Areas Of The Ground:
Adults £16
Over 60's/Under 18's £8

■ Programme & Fanzines
Official Programme £2.

■ Record Attendance
43,024 v Glasgow Rangers,
Scottish Cup, February 1953.

■ Average Attendance
2005-2006: 3,797 (Division One)

■ Did You Know?
The Bob Shankly Stand is named after a former manager of Dundee and brother of the legendary Bill Shankly, of Liverpool fame.

Gretna

Raydale Park

Ground Name: Raydale Park
Capacity: 2,200
Address: Dominion Road,
Gretna, DG16 5AP
Telephone No: 01461-337-602
Fax No: 01461-338-047
Pitch Size: 105 x 68m
Year Ground Opened: 1946
Club Nickname: Black & Whites or
Borderers
Home Kit Colours: Black & White

Official Web Site:
www.gretnafootballclub.co.uk

Unofficial Website:
Gretna Mad (Footy Mad Network) –
www.gretna-mad.co.uk

■ What's The Ground Like?
The ground is on the small side and is predominantly terracing, with half the ground being largely for standing supporters. Both of these areas are quite small, being only a few feet deep. One end, known as the "Long Stand", is a simple covered terrace which is for home supporters. This has a number of small supporting pillars running across the front of it and four white flag poles on its roof. Opposite was a small open terrace, which has now been replaced by a temporary seated

stand which is allocated to away fans. On one side is the Ewart Engineering (Main) Stand, which is a small covered, all seated stand. Opposite is another simple covered area, which on one side is terrace and on the other there are just two rows of seating. Again there is a row of supporting pillars along the entire length of the stand. There is a Club Shop located inside the ground on the Main Stand side of the ground. The ground is pleasantly well situated with lots of trees surrounding it, although the newish-looking set of floodlights (four running down each side of the ground), do little to enhance it.

■ What Is It Like For Visiting Supporters?
Gretna offers a pleasant and hassle free day out, although the portaloos available in the away end leave a lot to be desired. However, at least now more away fans can be admitted to the ground now that the away end capacity has been increased, after the Club erected a temporary seated stand, at the away end of the ground. Peter Llewellyn adds; 'Make sure to try the pies as they are excellent'.

■ Where To Drink?
There is a supporters 'Club House' at the edge of the car park, which allows in away supporters. Jim Burnett adds; 'Other pubs which welcome away fans are The Royal Stewart on Glasgow Road & The Crossways Inn on Annan Road. Both of these bars

are around a ten-minute walk away from the ground'.

■ How To Get There & Where To Park?

From the M74 take the B7076 towards Gretna. Then turn onto the B721 which will take you through Gretna itself. After crossing Central Avenue (which has a few shops along it), take the 3rd left into Dominion Road for the ground. There is a sign at the end of Dominion Road pointing in the direction of the Club and Sunday market. There is a large car park adjacent to the ground, which costs £1.

■ By Train

The ground is around a 15-minute walk away from Gretna Green station. When leaving the platform follow the sign for Gretna (not Gretna Green). You will then walk through a tunnel below the train track and onto a path through a field. Once you have walked through the field walk straight through the housing estate until you find a church on you right hand side. Turn right and walk down this road for about 5 minutes until you see a sign for Gretna Market, walk down this road and you will find the ground situated within the car park. Thanks to David Grant for supplying the directions.

■ Local Rivals

Queen Of The South & Annan Athletic.

■ Admission Prices

Seating:
Adults £14,
Concessions £7.

Terrace:
Adults £12,
Concessions £6.

■ Programme

Official Programme £2.

■ Record Attendance

3,000 v Dundee United
FA Cup 3rd Round, January 17th 2005.

■ Average Attendance

2005-2006: 1,304 (Division Two)

■ Did You Know?

That from its formation in 1946 until the 2002/03 season the Club used to compete in English non-League football.

Ground Name:	New Douglas Park
Capacity:	5,300 (all seated)
Address:	Cadzow Avenue, Hamilton, Lanarkshire ML3 0FT
Telephone No:	01698-383-650
Fax No:	01698-285-422
Pitch Size:	115 x 75 yards
Year Ground Opened:	2001
Club Nickname:	The Accies
Home Kit Colours:	Red & White

Official Web Site:
www.acciesfc.co.uk

Unofficial Website:
None at present.

■ What's The Ground Like?

At long last the club has its own home, after spending seven years of ground sharing with other Clubs, since giving up their Douglas Park ground in 1994. The new ground, which is near to the former site of the original Douglas Park (now a Sainsburys Supermarket), was opened in time for the 2001/02 season and even though it currently has only two sides, it is at least somewhere the fans can call home, once again. Both stands are covered all seated stands, at one side and at one end of the pitch. They are unusual, in terms of modern stands, in that they are both raised above pitch level, which means that spectators have to climb a set of stairs to reach the seated area. There are also four striking floodlight pylons in each corner of the ground.

■ What Is It Like For Visiting Supporters?

Away fans are normally housed in one section of the Main Stand, where the view of the action is good. For those clubs with a larger following then the North Stand will be allocated instead. Alan Redman, a visiting Morton supporter adds; 'there is plenty of legroom in the North Stand, but wrap up well in winter as, being as the ground is largely open, the wind blows right through it'.

Ross Clark, a Hamilton fan informs me; 'Despite having only the two stands at the moment, it's possible to make quite a lot of noise from either stand. You kind of forget that there's nothing on the other side of the pitch until the ball goes out and it takes the ball boys far too long to retrieve the ball from the far wall. (a few impatient staff have taken to just punting a new one on almost as soon as it happens). The evening matches in the dark have been better for atmosphere'.

■ Where To Drink?

There is a Social Club in the Main Stand where away fans are welcome. Whilst Craig Irvine recommends; 'The Clansman Bar in nearby Burnbank, which is a decent pub. There are two other local bars at Peacock Cross; the Silver Tassie and Harvies. The Chambers at the court is also not bad.' Jim Galloway adds; 'The Railway Club in

Clydesdale Street is a good place to go for a drink before the game and non members are welcome on matchdays'.

How To Get There & Where To Park?

Leave the M74 at Junction 5, and follow the signs for Hamilton. You will pass the racecourse on your left and a large fire station on your right. At the first set of traffic lights, turn right into Caird Street. On your left will appear a fair sized car park, which you can park in and embark on the 10-minute walk to the ground. Or if you continue along Caird Street, you turn right, just before the traffic lights (and bingo hall) into New Park Street. You will come to the ground entrance on your left.

There is no parking available for supporters at the ground itself, unless you are a club official, or have a valid disabled permit. However, due to limited space even these should be pre-booked with the Club.

By Train

The ground is only a few minutes walk from Hamilton West station, which is served by trains from Glasgow Central. Please note that Hamilton Central station is quite far away from the ground.

Local Rivals

Motherwell.

Admission Prices

Adults £14,
Concessions £6.

Programme

Official Programme: Free on admission!

Record Attendance

At New Douglas Park:
4,280 v Sunderland (Friendly match played in 2001)

At Douglas Park
28,690 v Hearts (1937)

Average Attendance

2005-2006: 1,717 (Division One)

Did You Know?

The Club got its name from the local Hamilton Academy school.

Ground Name: Almondvale Stadium
Capacity: 10,000 (all seated)
Address: Livingston,
West Lothian, EH54 7DN
Telephone No: 01506-417-000
Fax No: 01506-418-888
Pitch Size: 110 x 76 yards
Year Ground Opened: 1995
Undersoil Heating: Yes
Club Nickname: Livi Lions
Home Kit Colours: Amber & Black

Official Web Site:
www.livingstonfc.co.uk

Unofficial Websites:
LiviLions - www.livilions.co.uk
Livi Ultras (Footy Mad Network) - www.liviultras.com

What's The Ground Like?
This purpose built stadium opened in 1995. It is a small, compact but smart-looking ground. All four stands are of roughly the same height and two corners of the ground are filled with covered seating. There are open corners to the ground on either side of the West Stand, at one side of the pitch, which also has a few supporting pillars.

George Hobb, a visiting Hearts supporter adds, 'The club grew from the ashes of the former Meadowbank Thistle who played in Edinburgh, until in a move similar to NFL franchises, it was moved lock stock and barrel to Livingston. Efforts to retain the name were in vain as the major players saw this as an opportunity to get the town on Scotland's soccer map. What has been achieved in a short time is a minor miracle. Third division to Premier League, crowds quadrupled and most importantly a sound foundation has been put in place. Plus the ground is so neat, that you half expect the players to be on plastic bases and flicked around on the pitch!'

What Is It Like For Visiting Supporters?
Away fans are located in the North Stand and the North East corner of the ground. Up to 4,000 fans can be accommodated in this area. Livingston are a family orientated club and hence you are likely to have an enjoyable and relaxing day out. There is also a small band of drummers and trumpeters in the Livingston crowd who try to raise the atmosphere throughout the game, with a number of well known tunes. Aidan Hegarty, a visiting Dundee United supporter adds; 'visitors should be aware that the club operates a zero tolerance policy towards foul or abusive language, so try to be on your best behaviour'.

Where To Drink?
George Hobbs informs me, 'try The Granary up from the Main Stand, that was quite popular on my visit'. Whilst up at the McArthur Glen Shopping Centre, there is a Wetherspoons pub, although no football colours are allowed to be displayed.

How To Get There & Where To Park?

Livingston is situated approximately 18 miles west of Edinburgh and easily accessible from the M8 motorway. The stadium is fairly well signposted around the town. The following directions from the M8 are not necessarily the quickest, but they are fairly straightforward to follow.

Leave the M8 at Junction 3 and take the A899 towards Livingston. Leave the this road when you reach the large roundabout that is the junction with the A71 (Bankton Road). Turn right onto the A71 and at the next island turn right into Alderstone Road (sign posted town centre). Go straight across three roundabouts and then turn right at the second set of traffic lights and into the stadium approach road. There is a fair sized car park at the stadium, although it does cost a whopping £5 to park there!

By Train

There are two stations that are in reach of the ground. Livingston North & Livingston South. The North station is served by trains from Edinburgh and is about a fifteen-minute walk away from the ground. Whilst the South station receives trains from both Edinburgh and Glasgow and is about a 25-minute walk away from the ground.

Local Rivals

With being a relatively new club, local rivalries have yet to be firmly established. However, if the club maintains its current growth, then the Edinburgh clubs may be the focus of rivalry.

Admission Prices

Adults: £18
Concessions: £10

Programme

Official Programme £2.50

Record Attendance

10,112 v Rangers, Premier League, October 27th, 2001.

Average Attendance

2005-2006: 4,938 (Premier League)

Did You Know?

The smallest attendance recorded for a Livingston league match was just 223, who attended the game against Queens Park at Meadowbank Stadium in 1995. How times have now changed...

Partick Thistle

Firhill Stadium

Ground Name: Firhill Stadium
Capacity: 13,079 (10,887 seated)
Address: 80 Firhill Road,
Glasgow, G20 7AL
Telephone No: 0141-579-1971
Fax No: 0141-945-1525
Pitch Size: 111 x 76 yards
Year Ground Opened: 1909
Club Nickname: The Jags
Home Kit Colours: Red, Yellow & Black

Official Web Site:
www.ptfc.co.uk

Unofficial Websites:
Over Land & Sea -
http://www.chem.gla.ac.uk/~johnm/thistle/partick.html
The Harry Rags - www.theharrywraggs.co.uk
PTFC.net - www.ptfc.net

■ What's The Ground Like?
On one side of the ground is the impressive-
looking, Jackie Husband Stand. This is a large,
covered single-tiered stand. Opposite is the older
Main Stand, which has raised seating above pitch
level. This stand is covered and has a fair few
supporting pillars which may obstruct your view. It
was originally built in 1927. The stand looks a little
odd, as the lower end has been given over to what
look like administrative offices. As it is timber
framed, smoking is not permitted in the seated

area. At the North End of the ground is the new
North Stand, which replaced a former open terrace.
This all seated covered stand, originally only ran for
around two-thirds of the width of the pitch, but
has been extended during the Summer of 2003,
so that it now completely fills that end of the
ground. Opposite the South End is a classic-looking
open terrace, which is semi circular in shape.
This end is not used currently by the Club, who
intend to redevelop this terraced area at some
point in the future.

■ Future developments
The club have plans to re-develop the south end of
the stadium. This would include a 1,000 all seater
stand plus residential and office accommodation.
However, the club has yet to successfully obtain
planning permission to go ahead with this
development.

■ What Is It Like For Visiting Supporters?
Away Fans are primarily housed in the new North
Stand at one side of the pitch, where around 2,000
fans can be accommodated. The view of the
playing action and the facilities on offer are pretty
good. The good thing about this Stand, is that a
relatively few away supporters can make some
noise from it, contributing to a normally good
atmosphere within the ground. If demand requires
it, then the North part of the older Main Stand
can also be allocated to away fans. Otherwise
this classic-looking stand remains unused for
spectators.

Partick Thistle

Firhill holds a somewhat illustrious personal record for myself. Having had a few beers before the game, I unfortunately needed to find the gents half way through the first half. Just as I got in there, up went a roar from inside the ground, Partick had scored. Then on returning, just as I reached the bottom of the stairs, going back up into the stand. Partick scored again! So this is still my personal record of missing two goals with one pee! Of course, I took a fair bit of ribbing from the surrounding supporters as I returned to my seat. In a dull second half, there were plenty of suggestions from the fans around me, that perhaps I should work my goal magic, by going to the gents again!

Firhill is the only ground that I have come across on my extensive travels, that sells Pot Noodles from its refreshment areas (apart from pies etc...)

■ Where To Drink?

Jim McFarlane recommends the Munn's Vaults on Maryhill Road. This pub is only around a five-minute walk from the entrance to the away end and has a good mix of home and away support. Further down Maryhill Road towards the city centre, there is over on the right of the road the Woodside Inn, which also welcomes away fans.

■ How To Get There & Where To Park?

From The West:
Leave the M8 at Junction 17 and follow the A81, Maryhill Road towards Maryhill. Turn right into Firhill Road for the ground.

From The East:
Leave the M8 at Junction 16 and follow the A81, Maryhill Road towards Maryhill. Turn right into Firhill Road for the ground.

Street Parking (although don't be surprised if you are approached by a number of kids wanting to 'mind your car mister').

■ By Train/Underground

Maryhill Station is the closest train station to the ground, but it is still a fair walk away (20-25 minutes). It is served by trains from Glasgow Queens Street, but it may be best instead to use the Underground.

By Underground:
Richard Jones informs me; 'you can alight at two or three underground stations. Probably the easiest

is to get off at St. Georges Cross, and just head North up Maryhill Road until you see the stadium (in Firhill road just off Maryhill road). It should take around 10-15 minutes to walk. Another option is to get off at Kelvinbridge (this is slightly closer to Firhill than St. Georges Cross). Go up the stairs/escalators to Great Western Road, cross Great Western Road and turn to your right. Walk only a few metres until you come to North Woodside Road on your left. Walk down that road until you come to Maryhill Road. Turn left along Maryhill Road to get to the ground.

Alan McAulay adds, 'If you are looking to have a pre-match drink in Byres Road, then alight at Hillhead Underground Station. Most of the pubs are on the left hand side when you exit the station, although the very studenty Curlers Bar is right next to it. A better bet may be Tennents Bar, which is further down as it has more of a 'footy-friendly' atmosphere. To then get to the ground from Byres Road turn right out of Hillhead Station and go straight along past the library and Fopp records, then turn right again. Kelvinbridge station is on your right hand side, but below street level, so keep an eye out for it' then directions are as above.

■ Local Rivals
Clyde, Airdrie, St Mirren.

■ Admission Prices

All parts of the ground (Seating):
Adults - £13*,
Concessions £7

* For all ticket games this rises to £19.

■ Programme
Official Programme £2.

■ Record Attendance
49,838 v Rangers (1922)

■ Average Attendance
2005-2006: 2,610 (Division Two)

■ Did You Know?
That Firhill is the closest League Football Ground to Glasgow City Centre.

Ground Name: Palmerston Park
Capacity: 6,412 (3,509 seated)
Address: Dumfries, DG2 9BA
Telephone No: 01387-254-853
Fax No: 01387-240-470
Pitch Size: 112 x 73 yards
Year Ground Opened: 1919*
Club Nickname: Doonhamers
Home Kit Colours: Royal Blue & White

Official Web Site:
www.qosfc.com

Unofficial Websites:
Only One Team In The Bible - www.qosfan.co.uk
Queen Of The South Mad (Footy Mad Network) –
www.queenofthesouth-mad.co.uk

■ What's The Ground Like?

Palmerston Park is a great-looking traditional
ground, with a nice blend of new and old stands.
On one side of the ground is the relatively new
Galloway News (East) Stand. This smart-looking,
all seated single-tier stand, is covered and runs the
full length of the pitch. Opposite is the Dumfries &
Galloway Grandstand, a classic-looking small
covered seated stand, that has a raised seated
area. It only runs for around half the length of the
pitch, straddling the half way line. There are small
portions of terracing at the front of the stand and
at either side. At one end is the Portland Drive
Terrace. This is a fair sized terrace, that is partly
covered (to the rear). The roof has a gable perched
upon it, which features a traditional-looking clock.
The only downside to the stadium is the Terregles
Street End, a small open terrace no longer used

that has fallen into disrepair. The ground also has a
striking set of floodlights.

■ What Is It Like For Visiting Supporters?

Away fans are located in the relatively new
Galloway News (East) Stand, which is shared
with home supporters. Around half this stand is
allocated, which is around 1,100 seats. If demand
requires it, then the whole of this stand can be
allocated, taking the total allocation to 2,200.
The facilities in this stand and view of the action
are pretty good and even a small amount of away
supporters can really generate some noise from it.

R Shields, a visiting Clyde supporter informs me;
'This is perhaps one of the best, if not the best
days out in the first division. A hospitable ground,
good facilities, placed in a town that is enjoyable
to visit. Queens are good competition, and if I had
to single out a favourite away game, then this
would be it!' Whilst Philip Addison, a visiting
Darlington supporter adds; 'The ground was a
mixture of a new stand, an updated old stand and
old terraces. It felt like a throwback to watching
football in years gone by. The atmosphere was
lively, especially at times when a bagpipe player
was blowing'.

■ Where To Drink?

There is a bar at the ground, at the rear of the
West Stand. This is called the Palmerston Lounge
Bar and away fans are welcome. The nearest bar, is
the Spread Eagle Inn, which is about a five-minute
walk away. Around the corner from this bar are a
number of others including the Devorgilla and the
Globe.

■ How To Get There & Where To Park?

Approaching Dumfries from the North or East you

will reach the A75 Dumfries by pass. Follow signs or Kilmarnock/Stranraer and when you reach the roundabout, that is the junction with the A76 Glasgow Street) turn left towards Dumfries. Go over a couple of roundabouts and when you reach a T-junction (where you can see the Spread Eagle Inn), with a set of traffic lights, turn right at the lights onto the A780. A short way down this road turn right into Terregles Street for the ground. There is a fair amount of parking at the 'Ice Bowl' behind the Galloway News (East Stand), otherwise there is some street parking available.

■ By Train
Dumfries is served by trains from Glasgow & Carlisle. The ground is just over a mile away from the ground and should take about 15-20 minutes to walk. When you arrive by train you will see an imposing hotel right in front of you and behind it is a street called Lovers Walk. Turn right along Lovers Walk until you reach Academy Street. Continue along Academy Street bearing right past Burns Statue on to Buccleuch Street. Continue until you pass over Buccleuch Street Bridge then on to Galloway Street. Continue then turn right on to Terregles Street and about 200 yards further on is Palmerston Park.

Thanks to Eric Fisher, for providing the directions.

■ Local Rivals
Stranraer, Gretna & Ayr United.

■ Admission Prices

The Dumfries and Galloway Standard Stand
Adults £12,
No concessions

All other areas of the ground:
Adults £10,
Concessions £6

■ Programme
Official Programme £2.

■ Record Attendance
26,552 v Hearts,
Scottish Cup 3rd Round, February 23rd, 1952.

■ Average Attendance
2005-2006: 1,804 (Division One)

■ Did You Know?
The Club's nickname 'Doonhamers' comes from the local Dumfries saying 'Doon Hame' meaning 'Down Home'. 'Doonhamers' is therefore used to describe someone from Dumfries.

*   The ground has been home to the Club since 1919 and although developed by the Club, football had been played on the land since the 1870s.

Ross County

Victoria Park

Ground Name: Victoria Park
Capacity: 5,800 (2,800 seats)
Address: Jubilee Road,
Dingwall, IV15 9QZ
Telephone No: 01349-860-860
Fax No: 01349-866-277
Pitch Size: 100 x 75 yards
Year Ground Opened: 1929
Club Nickname: The County
Home Kit Colours: Navy Blue & White

Official Web Site:
www.rosscountyfootballclub.co.uk

Unofficial Websites:
The Jail Ender - www.thejailender.com

■ What's The Ground Like?
Although originally opened in 1929, the ground
has a newish feel about it, as significant
investment has been put into it in recent years.
The West Stand at one side of the pitch is an
attractive-looking all seated, covered stand, with a
row of executive boxes running across the back.
Part of this stand is given to away supporters. This
stand was originally opened in 1991, but was
extended in 2000, so that the stand now runs for
the whole length of the pitch. Opposite is the
East Stand, a small, covered, all-seated stand,
which was built in 1995. Both ends are similar
sized terraces. The home end, the South Terrace
(known locally as the Jail End) is covered, whilst
the away end, the North Terrace is uncovered.

■ What Is It Like For Visiting Supporters?
Away fans are primarily housed in the North
Terrace at one end of the ground. This area is
uncovered, so be prepared to get wet. A better bet
may be to head for one of the seats allocated to
away supporters in the West Stand, at one side of
the pitch, as these are covered. Please note though
that entrance to the ground is by ticket only, no
cash is accepted at the turnstiles. You will need to
buy your ticket from the ticket office, which is the
dark red portacabin which is situated by the car
park across the road from the West Stand.

■ Where To Drink?
The ground is five minutes walk away from the
town centre, where there are plenty of bars to
choose from. Scott Armstrong recommends; 'The
Mallard is a good friendly pub with excellent bar
food. It is located by the railway station and only
300 yards from Victoria Park'.

■ How To Get There & Where To Park?

Take the A835 into Dingwall. On approaching the centre, turn right into Park Street and then right onto the High Street. Continue down the High Street and straight on into Ferry Road. The ground is down on the right. If you get lost, follow signs for the railway station, as the ground is right by it. There is a car park at the ground, which costs £2.

■ By Train

Dingwall train station is only a few minutes walk away from the ground.

■ Local Rivals

Inverness Caledonian Thistle.

■ Admission Prices

Seating:
Adults £14,
Concessions £6.

Terrace:
Adults £12,
Concessions £5.

■ Programme

Official Programme £1.50.

■ Record Attendance

8,000 v Rangers (1966)

■ Average Attendance

2005-2006: 2,302 (Division One)

■ Did You Know?

That with a capacity of 6,000, the ground holds more that the entire population of the town of Dingwall that it is situated in.

Ground Name: McDiarmid Park
Capacity: 10,673 (all seated)
Address: Crieff Road,
Perth, PH1 2SJ
Telephone No: 01738-459-090
Fax No: 01738-625-771
Ticket Office: 01738-455-000
Pitch Size: 115 x 75 yards
Year Ground Opened: 1989
Club Nickname: The Saints
Home Kit Colours: Blue & White

Official Web Site:
www.stjohnstonefc.co.uk

Unofficial Website:
Temple Of Saints -
www.grange.demon.co.uk/saints/sjfc.htm
We Are Perth Forum - www.weareperth.co.uk/forum/

■ What's The Ground Like?
The ground was built in 1989, and replaced the former home of Muirton Park. The ground consists of four single-tiered stands, that are covered and all seated. Three of the stands are of the same height, with the Main Stand at one side of the ground, being a little taller. Overall the ground has a tidy compact feel to it. There is an electric scoreboard situated in one corner of the ground.

■ What Is It Like For Visiting Supporters?
For the majority of games this season, only both sides of the stadium will be open. Away fans are normally housed in the North End of the Main (West) Stand, where the facilities and view of the playing action are good. For those games where the away side has a large travelling support then the North Stand will be allocated where up to 2,000 fans can be accommodated.

■ Where To Drink?
The closest pub is the 208 Bar which is on Crieff Road about 300 yards away from the ground. The bar is popular with both home and away supporters.

■ How To Get There & Where To Park?

From The South:
Follow the A9 towards Perth and then on reaching Perth continue on the A9 towards Inverness. You will see the ground on your right and at the next roundabout you need to turn back on yourself and then take the slip road to the ground. The ground is well signposted around the local area.

There is a good sized car park (£2) at the ground, which can be quite time-consuming at the end of the match to get out of.

■ By Train
Perth train station is nearly three miles away from the ground, which is really too far to walk. Best bet is to grab a taxi.

■ Local Rivals
Dundee United, Dundee & Falkirk.

St Johnstone

Admission Prices

Home Fans:

Main Stand
Adults £18,
Senior Citizens/Under 18's £10

East Stand
Adults £16,
Senior Citizens £5,
Under 18's £4

Away Fans:

Main Stand -
Adults £18,
Senior Citizens/Under 18's £10

Programme
Official Programme £2.

Record Attendance
10,721 v Rangers, February 26th, 1990.

Average Attendance
2005-2006: 2,667 (Division One)

Did You Know?
That the club derives its name from St.John's Toun (Town), the ancient name for the city of Perth.

Ground Name: Recreation Park
Capacity: 3,100 (400 seated)
Address: Clackmannan Rd, Alloa, FK10 1RY
Telephone No: 01259-722-695
Fax No: 01259-210-886
Pitch Size: 110 x 75 yards
Year Ground Opened: 1895
Club Nickname: Wasps
Home Kit Colours: Gold & Black

Official Web Site:
www.alloaathletic.co.uk

Unofficial Websites:
The Return Of The Duffle - www.alloasupporters.org.uk
Alloa Athletic Mad (Footy Mad Network) –
www.alloaathletic-mad.co.uk

What's The Ground Like?
The ground is predominantly terracing, with terraces behind each goal and along one side of the pitch. There is an unusual-looking Main Stand on the other side of the ground. This covered, all seated stand, runs for around half the length of the pitch. The seating is raised above pitch level and there are a number of supporting pillars, plus a couple of floodlight pylons which could impede your view. Opposite there is a small covered area in the middle of the terrace towards the rear.

Again it has a number of supporting pillars running across the front of it, with a row of four floodlight pylons in front, running along the perimeter of the pitch. Recently the club have embarked on covering the Clackmannan Road End of the ground, with a small roofing structure, to at least give home fans some protection in poor weather.

What Is It Like For Visiting Supporters?
With the covering of the Clackmannan Road End of the ground, the Club have decided to now enforce segregation for games. Therefore away fans will now be predominantly housed in the Railway End of the ground and/or the Hilton Road Terrace running down one side of the pitch. Both these terraces are open to the elements, so be prepared to get wet. Normally a relaxing and enjoyable visit.

Where To Drink?
There are no bars in the immediate vicinity of the ground. Duncan Condie informs me; 'I believe that The Bank and The Thistle are good pubs for a pre-match drink. Both are in the town centre about 5-10 minutes walk along Clackmannan Road'. Also in the town centre at Junction Place is the Thistle Bar which is attached to the Maclay's Thistle Brewery. So you would hope to get a great pint there!

How To Get There & Where To Park?
The ground is easy to find at it is located on the A907, on the West side of town. If approaching

om Stirling, continue on the A907 through the
entre of Alloa and you will eventually reach the
 round on your left. Street Parking.

By Train

ne nearest station is in Stirling which is around
even miles away. Mark Nixon adds; 'There are a
umber of buses that leave Stirling Bus Station
vhich is adjacent to the railway station) which go
ast Alloa's ground or to Alloa Town Centre':

o 14 to Dunfermline - hourly service, right past
ne ground.
o 60 to Clackmannan - every 20 minutes, right
ast the ground.
o 63 to Alloa - every 20 minutes, to Alloa town
entre.

Local Rivals

tirling Albion.

Admission Prices

Seating:
Adults £11,
Concessions £6.

Terrace:
Adults £10,
Concessions £5.

Programme

)fficial Programme £1.50.

Record Attendance

13,000 v Dunfermline Athletic,
Scottish Cup, 3rd Round replay, February 26th,
1939.

Average Attendance

005-2006: 730 (Division Two)

Did You Know?

loodlights were first used at the ground in the
979-80 season.

Ayr United

Somerset Park

Ground Name: Somerset Park
Capacity: 10,243 (seated 1,549)
Address: Tryfield Place,
Ayr, KA8 9NB
Telephone No: 01292-263-435
Fax No: 01292-281-314
Pitch Size: 110 x 72 yards
Year Ground Opened: 1896*
Club Nickname: The Honest Men
Home Kit Colours: White & Black

Official Web Site:
None At Present

Unofficial Website:
The Honest Page - www.honestpage.co.uk

■ What's The Ground Like?

A classic, traditional-looking ground that is predominantly terracing. Only one side has a seating area, in the old Main Stand, part of which dates back to 1924. This stand is covered and the seated area is raised above pitch level. There are also a few supporting pillars which could impede your view. This stand was extended sideways in 1989. In front of the stand are some small sections of terracing, the team dugouts and a small conservatory type structure, that looked to be used by the Police. On the other side is a large open terrace that extends around the corners of the ground. This area is split between home and away fans, who are segregated by a large fence running down the middle of it. At the back of the home fans section is a strange concrete box like structure that looks to have been built behind the existing

terrace. This appears to house a number of hospitality boxes that overlook the ground. Both ends are quite similar looking, as they are of roughly the same size and both are covered terracing. The home end, the Somerset Road end is partly covered (to the rear) medium sized terrace, which has a row of supporting pillars running across the front of it. Away fans are located in the opposite end in the Railway Terrace. The ground is completed with a striking set of four floodlight pylons, one located at each corner of the ground.

■ What Is It Like For Visiting Supporters?

Away fans are primarily located in the covered Railway End Terrace at one end of the ground, as well as some open terrace to either side of it. So visiting fans have a choice as to whether to view the action from either an end or side of the pitch and unless there is a huge travelling support you will normally get a good view of the playing action. With the away end being covered, a relatively small number of away fans can really create some noise, adding to the atmosphere. There are two refreshment kiosks in the away section serving the usual array of pies, hot dogs & burgers. Unfortunately though there is only one set of toilets that are right by the entrance turnstiles to the away end. I would have to say that the mens urinals looked as if they dated back to when the ground opened. I did notice on my visit that parts of the open terrace had a fair few white blobs all over them, thanks to the large local population of seagulls. It may be an idea to make sure you wear a hat if you use the open terrace!

Simon Lyndsay, a visiting Falkirk supporter adds 'This is my favourite away game. It is a great old fashioned ground. With good pubs, pies, great fish nd chips and I have never had a bit of bother here. The fans can have a go at one another during the game (loads of verbals), but walking away at the end, there never seems to be any assle. An enthusiastic two thumbs up from me for omerset Park'.

Where To Drink?

here are no bars in the immediate vicinity of the round. The nearest I could find was the Prince of Wales, which is about a five-minute walk away. t is a fair sized comfortable bar with a large screen elevision showing SKY Sports. This bar is situated n the A719 (Whitletts Road) going towards Ayr own centre. Otherwise, the town centre is about a ten-minute walk away from the ground, where here are plenty of good bars to be found.

How To Get There & Where To Park?

rom the A77 take the A719 (Whitletts Road) into Ayr. After passing the racecourse on your left, turn ight at the next set of traffic lights for the ground, r turn left to take you down to an unofficial car ark. Turning right will take you into Burnett errace, then left into Hawkhill Avenue and then ight into Somerset Road. The ground is down on he left. There is plenty of parking to be found round the ground.

By Train

Ayr station is a ten-minute walk away from the ground. Exit the station through the back entrance to the left as you come off the platform, over the ootbridge) and turn left once outside. Walk up to he roundabout at the fire station, and go straight ahead at the roundabout, past the left hand side f the Civic Theatre. continue up this road (Craigie Road) to the traffic lights at the top. Go straight across again at this junction, then take a left and a ight and you're there. Away fans walk to the left, behind the Main Stand. Thanks to Ruaridh Watson or providing the directions.

Callum McCabe adds; 'Newton-On-Ayr station s closer to the ground than Ayr main station, although not as many trains stop there. Go up the hill from the station onto the main Allison Street A79). Turn right along Allison Street and then cross over to the other side of the road. Continue along Allison Street for a short distance and just before the the bridge where the road crosses the railway, turn left into McCall's Avenue. Go all the way up this road until you cross a railway bridge, and then turn right into Somerset

Road. The ground is at the bottom of this road on the right'.

Local Rivals
Kilmarnock.

Admission Prices

Seating:
Adults £14,
Concessions £10.

Terrace:
Adults £10,
Concessions £5.

Programme
Official Programme £1.50

Record Attendance
25,225 v Rangers, 1969.

Average Attendance
2005-2006: 1,272 (Division Two)

Did You Know?
The Club's nickname comes from a line in a famous poem called Tam O'Shanter by Robert Burns; 'Auld Ayr, wham ne'er a town surpasses, for "honest men" and bonny lasses'.

* The present Somerset Park ground overlies part of the original Somerset Park ground which dates back to 1888.

Brechin City

Glebe Park

Ground Name: Glebe Park
Capacity: 3,960 (Seated 1,519)
Address: Trinity Rd, Brechin, Angus, DD9 6BJ
Telephone No: 01356-622-856
Fax No: 01356-625-524
Pitch Size: 110 x 67 yards
Year Ground Opened: 1919
Club Nickname: The City
Home Kit Colours: Red & White

Official Web Site:
www.brechincity.co.uk

Unofficial Website:
Brechin City Mad (Footy Mad Network) –
www.brechincity-mad.co.uk

■ What's The Ground Like?

It is a long time since I have visited a ground with such charm and character as Glebe Park. The Main Stand is overlooked by a church spire, whilst opposite a tall, well tended hedge borders the entire length of the open side. This side has a small open terrace only a couple of steps high and there are a number of floodlight pylons running down the front of it. The Main Stand is a small but tall, all-seated and covered stand, which straddles the half way line. You would think at first glance that this was quite an old stand, especially as it has a floodlight protruding from its roof, but in actual fact it was built in 1981 and replaced a similar-looking wooden stand. At one end is the

Cemetery End terrace, which is covered and has a number of supporting pillars. Opposite, is the latest addition to the ground, the smart-looking Trinity Road Stand. Built in the early 1990's, it is a covered all seated stand, which seats nearly 1,000 spectators. It is unusual, in being setback some distance from the pitch and sits upon a raised bank.

■ What Is It Like For Visiting Supporters?

The ground is a pleasure to visit and a friendly welcome awaits most visitors. The ground is maintained to a high standard and the staff and fans have real pride in their club. If you get the chance, make your way to the rear of the Cemetery Terrace, where in true Hollywood style, supporters have been invited to have individual plaques with their names on, set in concrete. Plus the supporters have also been allowed to place their hand prints in the concrete, giving it that Hollywood look. Supporters are not normally segregated for games and both sets of fans tend to try and out-sing one another in the Cemetery End. If fans are to be segregated, say for a big cup game, then away fans will normally find that the Trinity Road Stand has been allocated to them. Neil Stapleton adds; 'If you get the chance, sample the soup on sale inside the ground, it is excellent'.

■ Where To Drink?

Calum MacLennan informs me; 'There is the Stables Bar which is good for a pre-match pint. This is only a five minute walk away from the ground. As you come out of the ground entrance, turn left and go down to the roundabout.

o straight across the roundabout and at
1cConnachys Tyre Centre turn right and the pub is
ıst there'. Otherwise there is the Springfield which
, a similar distance away. As you come out of the
round again turn left, and at the roundabout turn
ght, then right again into Cookston Road. The
pringfield can be seen up on the right.

How To Get There & Where To Park?

rom the the A90 take the B966 towards Brechin
f coming from the South, ignore the first Brechin
ırn off on the A90, the A935, and continue
lorthwards). Continue along the B966 and you
vill come to the ground on your left. The entrance
5 quite small between some houses and is
ıdicated by a small Glebe Park sign. There is a
mall free car park at the ground which holds
round fifty vehicles, otherwise street parking.

By Train

here is no train station in Brechin itself. The
iearest station is in Montrose which is eight miles
way. You can either then take a taxi to the
jround, or catch a bus to Brechin.

Local Rivals

Montrose, Forfar.

Admission Prices

All Areas Of The Ground:
Adults £12,
OAP's/Juveniles £6,
Parent & Child £15.

For games where the fans are segregated,
visitors in the Trinity Road Stand are
charged as follows:

Adults £13,
OAP's/Juveniles £7,
Parent & Child £16.

Programme
Official Programme £1.50

Record Attendance
8,122 v Aberdeen,
Scottish Cup 3rd Round, February 3rd, 1973.

Average Attendance
2005-2006: 770 (Division One)

Did You Know?
Glebe Park is the only football ground in Europe
which has a hedge surrounding its perimeter.

Cowdenbeath

Central Park

Ground Name: Central Park
Capacity: 5,268 (Seated 1,622)
Address: Cowdenbeath,
Fife, KY4 9QQ
Telephone No: 01383-610-166
Fax No: 01383-512-132
Pitch Size: 107 x 66 yards
Year Ground Opened: 1917
Club Nickname: Cowden or Blue Brazil
Home Kit Colours: Royal Blue & White

Official Web Site:
www.cowdenbeathfc.com

Unofficial Websites:
Supporters Club –
www.cowdenbeath.free-online.co.uk/suppclub
Cowdenbeath.net - www.cowdenbeath.net

■ What's The Ground Like?
The ground is also used from time to time for motor sport events. This means that around the oval grass football playing area, at the front of the spectator areas, there is a fair sized tarmac track, plus a meshed safety fence. It is largely an open stadium with three sides having small open terraces. Only on the North Side of the stadium is there a covered Main Stand. Or really I should say Main Stands as there are two, as an older and newer structure, sit side by side. This is because the original old Main Stand was partly destroyed by fire in 1992 and a new structure was constructed beside the remnants of the old stand. Both are covered and all seated and have a row of floodlight pylons at the front of them, which could affect your view.

■ What Is It Like For Visiting Supporters?
For most games there is no segregation of supporters. If segregation needs to be enforced, then the terraces at both the South & East sides are allocated to away fans. The oval stock car track means that supporters using the end terrace are set rather far back from the action. For this reason supporters tend to congregate on either side of the ground, where you are a bit closer to the pitch. As the perimeter wall surrounding the stadium is not that high, you can often see a few dotted faces, peering over it and watching the game for nothing!

■ Where To Drink?
There is a small bar at the stadium itself, which is both popular with home and away supporters, plus there is also the nearby Park Bar which is also quite popular. Otherwise there are a number of other bars located on or around the nearby High St.

■ How To Get There & Where To Park?
The ground is located in the centre of the town, beside the High Street, however it is not easily visible when driving along the High Street itself.

Leave the M90 at Junction 3 and take the A92 towards Kirkcaldy. Then take the A909 into Cowdenbeath, which then leads into the High Street. After a short distance along the High Street there is a small parking sign entitled 'Central Park' which points left down a small road for the ground. If you miss the sign (as I did), continue further up the High Street and turn left into Stenhouse Street where there is an overflow car park used on matchdays. There is also a fair sized car park at the ground as well, which is free to use.

By Train
Cowdenbeath station is only five minutes walk from the ground and is served by trains from Edinburgh.

Local Rivals
East Fife.

Admission Prices

All areas of the ground:
Adults £9,
Concessions £4.

Programme
Official Programme £1.

Record Attendance
25,586 v Glasgow Rangers,
League Cup Quarter Final,
September 21st, 1949.

Average Attendance
2005-2006: 471 (Division Three)

Did You Know?
The Club were originally nicknamed the Miners, as at one time there was a mining pit adjacent to the ground.

Ground Name:	Station Park
Capacity:	4,602 (Seated 739)
Address:	Carseview Road, Forfar, Angus, DD8
Telephone No:	01307-463-576
Fax No:	01307-466-956
Pitch Size:	115 x 69 yards
Year Ground Opened:	1888
Club Nickname:	Loons
Home Kit Colours:	Sky Blue & Navy Blue

Official Web Site:
www.forfarathletic.co.uk

Unofficial Websites:
The Loonatic - www.theloonatic.co.uk
Loons Mad (Footy Mad Network) - www.loons-mad.co.uk

What's The Ground Like?
The ground is predominantly terracing, with terraces behind each goal and along one side of the pitch. The terraces at each end of the ground are not covered and are open to the elements. At one end is the small East Terrace, whilst opposite is the larger West Terrace. The latter is unusual in being taller on one side than the other. On one side of the ground is the Main Stand, which is a traditional-looking covered, seated stand. The seating is raised above pitch level and there are a number of supporting pillars at its front. This stand only runs for around half the length of the pitch. The team dugouts are located in front of this stand. On the other side is a small

covered terrace that runs the full length of the pitch. This stand looks relatively new and has a number of small floodlights protruding from its roof. There is quite a slope to the pitch that runs down across the ground from the West Terrace down to the East Terrace.

What Is It Like For Visiting Supporters?
Normally segregation of supporters is not in force, so most away fans tend to head for the covered South Terrace. If segregation takes place, then the open West Terrace is allocated to away supporters plus part of the Main Stand. The facilities are fairly basic around the ground, but as you would expect the bridies are pretty good!

Where To Drink?
The nearest bar is the Caledonian Bar in North Street. There is also the Plough Inn on Market Street. There are also a number of bakeries selling more of the legendary Forfar Bridies.

How To Get There & Where To Park?
The ground is located right on the outskirts of town. In fact the Main Stand, backs onto fields. From the A90 take the A926 towards Forfar. At the T-junction turn right into Brechin Road, then turn left into Market Street and then 2nd left into Carseview Road for the ground. There is only limited parking available at the ground, otherwise there is the nearby Muir Street car park or street parking.

By Train
Even though the ground is called Station Park, there is in fact no railway station in Forfar itself. The nearest stations are in Dundee or Arbroath, that are both around 14 miles away!

Local Rivals
Brechin, Arbroath & Montrose.

Admission Prices

All Areas Of The Ground:
Adults £10,
Concessions £5.

Programme
Official Programme £1.

Record Attendance
10,780 v Glasgow Rangers,
Scottish Cup 2nd Round, February 2nd, 1970.

Average Attendance
2005-2006: 545 (Division Two)

Did You Know?
The Club's nickname "Loons" is derived from the local dialect 'Loon' which means a 'strapping young man' usually connected with agriculture.

Morton

Cappielow Park

Ground Name: Cappielow Park
Capacity: 11,100 (Seated 5,741)
Address: Sinclair Street,
Greenock, PA15 2TY
Telephone No: 01475-723-571
Fax No: 01475-781-084
Pitch Size: 110 x 71 yards
Year Ground Opened: 1879
Club Nickname: Ton
Home Kit Colours: Royal Blue & White

Official Web Site:
www.gmfc.net

Unofficial Website:
Supporters Trust - www.gmst.org.uk

■ What's The Ground Like?
Cappielow is a fair sized ground, full of character,
but beginning to show its age. However, with a
new Chairman on board, efforts are being made to
brighten up and improve the overall state of the
ground. The Grandstand on one side of the ground,
is a single-tiered, all seated stand, which has a
number of supporting pillars in front. On its roof

are a set of strikingly unusual floodlights, another
set of which are also on the stand opposite. The
Cowshed as it is known, is a classic-looking stand
and is unusual in the respect that it has seating at
the front of it and terracing at its rear. Both ends
are open to the elements. The Wee Dublin End, is a
former terrace, with white benches bolted onto it,
which makes it look out of place. This end is
normally not used on match days. Beyond can be
seen a large crane, which is reminiscent of the ship
building days on the Clyde. Opposite is the small
Sinclair Street Terrace, that has a small clock
behind it.

■ What Is It Like For Visiting Supporters?
Fans are housed in one side of the Grandstand,
towards the Dublin End of the ground. There are a
fair few pillars in this stand that may impede your
view and the leg room is on the tight side. For
larger games then the Wee Dublin End can also be
allocated for away fans to use. A visit to Cappielow
is normally a relaxed day out and the Morton fans
do their best to get behind their team.

■ Where To Drink?
The Norseman Bar is right by the ground and is
popular with both home and away fans. It can get

quite busy on matchdays, but it is still the favoured
pre-match venue.

How To Get There & Where To Park?

From Glasgow head on the M8 and then A8
towards Greenock (along which you get a fine view
of Castle Rock in Dumbarton). Follow the A8 into
Greenock and you will reach the ground on your
left. It's just after going under a bridge with
Picollo's fish & chip shop on the corner. There is a
car park opposite the main entrance, which is free,
otherwise street parking.

By Train

The nearest station to the ground is Cartsdyke
which lies on the Glasgow Central-Gourock line.
The journey from Glasgow takes around 40
minutes and then the ground is about a five-
minute walk from Cartsdyke Station.

Local Rivals

St Mirren and Dumbarton.

Admission Prices

Seating:
Adults £14,
Concessions £8,
Adult + 1 Child £17.

Terrace:
Adults £12,
Concessions £7,
Under 15's £3,
Adult + 1 Child £14.

Programme

Official Programme £1.50.

Record Attendance

23,500 v Celtic,
April 29th, 1922.

Average Attendance

2005-2006: 2,760 (Division Two)

Did You Know?

The Club got its name from the street that a
number of its original founders lived in -
Morton Terrace.

Peterhead

Balmoor Stadium

Ground Name: Balmoor Stadium
Capacity: 4,000 (seated 998)
Address: Lord Catto Park,
Peterhead, AB42 1EU
Telephone No: 01779-478-256
Fax No: 01779-490-682
Pitch Size: 105 x 70 yards
Year Ground Opened: 1997
Club Nickname: The Blue Toon
Home Kit Colours: Blue & White

Official Web Site:
www.peterheadfc.org.uk

Unofficial Website:
None At Present

■ What's The Ground Like?

Balmoor has two virtually identical stands that run down each side of the ground. Both these all seated stands are roughly of the same height and are covered. The seating areas are raised above pitch level, which means that supporters need to climb a small set of stairs at the front of the stand to access them. The West Stand has windshields at either side of it. Both ends of the ground are open and don't have any formal terracing.

Peterhead joined the Scottish Football League at the beginning of the 2000/2001 season. One of the reasons why they were invited to join the league, was certainly their move to the Balmoor Stadium, which was opened in 1997. Previously the Club played at Recreation Park, which was sold for redevelopment to Safeways.

■ What Is It Like For Visiting Supporters?

David Gray informs me; 'The Balmoor Stadium is a friendly place where away fans are always made welcome. There is normally no segregation, so opposing fans are always able to mix with each other'. Fred McIntosh, a visiting Forfar fan adds; 'On my last visit there was a form of segregation in force, as Forfar fans were directed to the far side of one stand but it was not very strictly enforced. Food now includes a fish pie at £1.50, which was very good!'. However, remember to wrap up well, as the ground itself is quite exposed and there is normally a cold biting wind coming off the North Sea.

■ Where To Drink?

There is a Social Club located in the rear of the Main Stand, which welcomes away supporters. Otherwise there are plenty of bars to be found in the centre of town, which is a ten minute walk away.

■ How To Get There & Where To Park?

The ground is located just out of town on the A982 Peterhead to Fraserburgh Road.

From The South:
From the A90 you can take the first exit for Peterhead (the A982). This will take you to the town centre where you continue following the A982 towards Fraserburgh. You will go past a swimming pool and will reach the ground on your left. There are around 200 car parking spaces at the ground, which are free.

By Train
The nearest railway station is in Aberdeen, which is some 32 miles away! Therefore this ground has the record of being furthest from a station than any other League team in Britain.

Local Rivals
Elgin City & Fraserburgh.

Admission Prices
Adults £10, Concessions £5.

Programme
Official Programme £2.

Record Attendance
At Balmoor Stadium:
2,158 v Aberdeen, Friendly July 22nd, 2003

At Recreation Park:
8,643 v Raith Rovers, 1987

Average Attendance
2005-2006: 691 (Division Two)

Did You Know?
The Club played at their previous ground Recreation Park for 106 years, before moving to Balmoor Stadium in 1997.

Raith Rovers

Starks Park

Ground Name: Starks Park
Capacity: 10,104 (all seated)
Address: Pratt Street, Kirkcaldy, KY1 1SA
Telephone No: 01592-263-514
Fax No: 01592-642-833
Pitch Size: 113 x 70 yards
Year Ground Opened: 1891*
Club Nickname: Rovers
Home Kit Colours: Navy Blue, White & Red

Official Web Site:
www.rrfc.co.uk

Unofficial Website:
Independent Supporters Trust - www.raithtrust.org.uk

■ What's The Ground Like?
The ground has benefited greatly with the redevelopment of both ends. These stands, the North & South Stands, are virtually identical. Both are good sized, single-tiered stands with windshields on either side and unusual floodlights protruding from their roofs. The North Stand is given to away supporters. On one side of the pitch is the Railway Stand, a small, covered, all seated stand. Opposite, must be one of the most unusual Main Stands in Scotland. It is a classic-looking old stand, that only runs for less then half the length of the pitch, but extends around one corner of the ground. It is a covered seated stand, the seating

area of which is raised above pitch level and has a number of supporting pillars. Even so, the stand oozes character, complete with a 'RRFC' gable on its roof. It is just unfortunate that the rest of this side of the ground is empty.

■ What Is It Like For Visiting Supporters?
Away fans are normally housed in the North Stand at one end of the ground. The angle of the stand is quite steep, ensuring a good view of the playing action. The facilities in this stand are also quite good. If there is only a small visiting support expected, then the South side of the Main Stand is allocated instead of the North End.

Andy Turner adds; 'The staff at the ground are welcoming and friendly. The folk who run the supporters shop, located in the south stand, personify the welcoming nature of the Club as a whole. I recently took a friend, a Plymouth fan for his first Scottish game and the lads at the shop gave him a commemorative programme as a souvenir. The Chancellor of the Exchequer, Gordon Brown is to be seen in the little old stand on occasions; apparently Gordon Brown sold programmes in his Kirkcaldy youth and has followed the club all his life'.

■ Where To Drink?
Martin Hart informs me; 'The Starks Bar is the nearest bar to the ground and is popular with both home and away supporters. However, it can get very busy on matchdays'. Andy Turner adds; 'Raith's

upport usually congregate at the Novar Bar in
Nicol Street. In my opinion though, the best boozer
in the town is the Harbour Bar. A regular CAMRA
award winner whose landlord brews his own
excellent ale as well as having wonderfully-kept
guest beers from around the UK. The pub is on the
seafront by the harbour area (hence the name)
next to Fife College Priory Campus. It's a fair
distance to the ground, but for those who fancy a
"bracing walk" it's a matter of a hike the length of
the seafront. You can still see the floodlights of the
'San Starko" in the distance.'

How To Get There & Where To Park?
Take the A921 into Kirkcaldy. Turn onto the B9157
(Pratt Street) for the ground. The ground is well
sign posted (football traffic) on entering the town.
Street Parking.

By Train
Kirkcaldy railway station is around a 15 minute
walk away from the ground. Exit the station via the
door at the top of the stairs on platform 2, then
turn left down the hill. Go right under the railway
bridge and at the mini roundabout turn left into
Abbotshall Road. This road (keeping the railway to
your left) eventually leads into Pratt Street and to
the ground.

Local Rivals
Dunfermline, Falkirk, Cowdenbeath & East Fife.

Admission Prices

Adults £12,
Concessions £6,
Pre-School Child Free (when accompanied by
an adult).

Programme
Official Programme £2.

Record Attendance
31,306 v Hearts (1953).

Average Attendance
2005-2006: 1,624 (Division Two)

Did You Know?
That the club named itself after the local Laird
(Lord) Raith and the ground was named after its
original owner Robert Stark.

* Although Raith Rovers took up residence in
1891, the ground had been used for some years
previously for football matches.

Stirling Albion

Forthbank Stadium

Ground Name: Forthbank Stadium
Capacity: 3,808 (Seated 2,508)
Address: Springkerse,
Stirling, FK7 7UJ
Telephone No: 01786-450-399
Fax No: 01786-448-400
Pitch Size: 110 x 74 yards
Year Ground Opened: 1993
Club Nickname: Albion or Binos/Beanos
Home Kit Colours: Red & White

Official Web Site:
None At Present

Unofficial Websites:
Unofficial Stirling Albion - www.stirlingalbion.com
Red Web - www.stirlingalbionfc.com
Supporters Trust - www.safcst.org.uk

■ What's The Ground Like?
This relatively new ground was opened in 1993,
after the Club moved from their original Annfield
home. The stadium comprises two seated stands,
on either side of the pitch and a small terrace at
either end. The largest of these stands is the West
Stand, which is a covered, single-tier, all seated
stand, that has some executive boxes running
across the back of it. Opposite is the similar-
looking East Stand, which is smaller that the West
Stand, not so much in height but in its overall
length. This is also covered, all seated and has a
Police Control Box situated at its rear. Away fans
are allocated this stand. The terraces at each end
of the stadium are almost identical. They are small

and uncovered box-like affairs, which are situated
well back from the pitch. These terraces are only
opened for the bigger games. Looking out beyond
the North Terrace there are some wonderful views
of the surrounding countryside. Outside of the
stadium there are a number of artificial pitches
behind the West Stand.

■ What Is It Like For Visiting Supporters?
Away fans are located in the East Stand at one
side of the pitch, where up to 1,000 fans can be
seated. This covered stand, has good facilities
and provides a good view of the playing action.
If demand requires it then a further 500 terrace
spaces can be provided in the South Terrace.

■ Where To Drink?
The stadium is on the very outskirts of town,
adjacent to a Retail Park, so there is not much
around. There is one pub called the Kerse Inn on
the Retail Park, which you will pass on your right
as you drive down to the stadium.

■ How To Get There & Where To Park?
Leave the M80 at Junction 9 and take the A91
towards Alloa. At the 4th roundabout turn left
and the ground is just down this road on the right.
There is a large car park at the ground which is free.

■ By Train
The stadium is around two miles away from Stirling
station, so best jump in a taxi. Otherwise it is a 35-
40 minute walk to it.

■ Local Rivals
Alloa.

Stirling Albion

Admission Prices

Seating:
Adults £10,
Concessions £6.

Terrace:
Adults £9,
Concessions £5.

Programme
Official Programme £1.

Record Attendance
At Annfield:
26,400 v Glasgow Celtic,
Scottish Cup, 4th Round, March 14th, 1959.

At Forthbank:
3,808 v Aberdeen,
Scottish Cup 4th Round, February 15th, 1996.

Average Attendance
2005-2006: 903 (Division Two)

Did You Know?
The Club previously played at Annfield Park,
which confused many on a quiz when faced with
the question, 'Apart from Liverpool who else plays
at a ground called Anfield?'

Ground Name: Stair Park
Capacity: 5,600 (1,830 Seated)
Address: London Road,
Stranraer, DG9 8BS
Telephone No: 01776-702-194
Fax No: 01776-702-194
Pitch Size: 110 x 70 yards
Year Ground Opened: 1907
Club Nickname: The Blues
Home Kit Colours: Royal Blue & White

Official Web Site:
www.stranraerfc.com

Unofficial Website:
Stranraer Mad (Footy Mad Network) –
www.stranraer-mad.co.uk

■ What's The Ground Like?
The ground is situated in a picturesque park, called Stair Park, hence the name of the ground. The Club have been playing in the park since in 1907, and the park itself even has a bandstand. The ground has seen a lot of improvements in recent years. In 1995 a new Main (South) Stand was constructed at one side of the pitch, built by Barr Construction, at a cost of £500,000. This smart-looking covered all seater stand, runs for roughly half the length of the pitch and straddles the half way line. There is a small amount of terracing on each side of the stand. From the back

of the Main Stand, you can enjoy good views of the surrounding area to the sea. On the other side is a small stand that is affectionately known as the 'Coo Shed'. This is a small covered stand, that has open terracing on either side of it, as well as a standing area in front. In the rear of this stand, are a number of rows of wooden benches. There are also a couple of supporting pillars in this stand. The Town End at one end of the ground is a small covered terrace, whilst at the other end, there is a small open terrace. At the back of this terrace are a number of trees and bushes, which gives the ground a rural look and I noticed a couple of kids seemed to be permanently employed during the game retrieving match balls from the undergrowth (the forwards were not having a good day on my visit!). There is also a small club shop within the ground, at one side of the Town End. It is also worth mentioning that the pitch is somewhat uneven in places.

■ What Is It Like For Visiting Supporters?
Fans are not normally segregated at Stair Park, but if required then away fans are given the Coo Shed and East Terrace, parts of the ground, where up to 2,000 fans can be accommodated. Away supporters tend to congregate in the Coo Shed as they can make themselves more vocally heard from this stand. The refreshment kiosks offer a selection of scotch pies and sausage rolls at 60p each as well as tea and coffee at 50p, per cup. I had an enjoyable afternoon out at Stair Park, however it is worth bearing in mind that when it's winter, you

should wrap up well as that wind can be biting, coming in off the sea.

Derek Hall adds; 'Just a few words about Stranraer. What a cracking little place. Nice pubs, nice chippie and nice guest houses. The best bit of the lot though is the friendly reception at the Stranraer FC Social Club - massively recommended'.

■ Where To Drink?

There is no club bar at the ground, however the ground is only a five minute walk away from the town centre where there are plenty of bars and eating establishments. As you leave Stair Park, turn left onto the main road to take you down to the town centre. The nearest bar is down on the right, in the Rudicot Hotel. This has a small quiet bar, which has a separate entrance on the side of the hotel. The bar serves a good pint of real ale (Deuchars IPA). If you continue down into the town centre then the next bar that you come to is 'The Pub' on the left hand side. This is a fair sized bar with TV's and a pool table. There is a chippy and cafe on the same side of the road. Colin Ferguson adds; 'probably the best bet for a drink before the game, is the Stranraer FC Social Club which is situated in North Strand St'.

■ How To Get There & Where To Park?

From The North:
Take the A77 from Glasgow down to Stranraer. This is not a particularly good road, so allow plenty of time for your journey. As you come into Stranraer either follow the road into the town centre and then turn left onto the A75 (Dumfries) and the ground and park are a short distance down this road on the right. Otherwise turn left from the A77, where the 'football traffic' is indicated by a sign. This takes you up to the A75 and again turn left and the ground and park are over on the right.

From The West:
Follow the A75 into Stranraer. As you pass a school on your right, you will come to the ground and park on your left.

There is free car parking in the park surrounding the ground.

■ By Train
Stranraer station is a fifteen minute walk away from the ground. From the railway station you should walk up to the ferry terminal building,

opposite North West Castle Hotel. Turn left walk about 150 yards to the 'Craig n Elder' Hotel. Turn right onto Stair Drive . At the end of Stair Drive turn left. This takes you onto London Road. Walk for about 200 yards and Stair Park is on the right hand side actually inside the public park. Thanks to J McCallum for providing the above directions.

■ Local Rivals
Queen Of The South & Ayr United.

■ Admission Prices

Main Stand (seating):
Adults £14,
Concessions £8.

Rest of ground (terrace):
Adults £12,
Concessions £6.

Children under 12 are admitted free when accompanied by an adult.

■ Programme
Official Programme £2.

■ Record Attendance
6,500 v Rangers, 1948.

■ Average Attendance
2005-2006: 630 (Division One)

■ Did You Know?
That Stranraer is closer to Belfast in Northern Ireland than Glasgow.

Ground Name:	Cliftonhill Stadium
Capacity:	2,496 (489 seated)
Address:	Main St, Coatbridge, Lanarkshir,. ML5 3RB
Telephone No:	01236-606-334
Fax No:	01236-606-334
Pitch Size:	110 x 72 yards
Year Ground Opened:	1919
Club Nickname:	Wee Rovers
Home Kit Colours:	Yellow & Red

Official Web Site:
None At Present

Unofficial Websites:
Albionrovers.com - www.albionrovers.com
Unofficial Albion Rovers - www.albionroversfc.tk

What's The Ground Like?

The ground is not one of the better in the League having only a small Main Stand and covered terrace at either side, with both ends being totally open and not used for spectators. The Main Stand is a strange looking affair, as at some point it has had an extension to its roof placed on the front. It has wooden seating to the rear and terracing to the front, with several supporting pillars which may impede your view. Opposite is the small, covered Albion Street Terrace, running about half the length of the pitch. Again, this simple stand has several supporting pillars. There is a cinder track that runs around the playing surface and at one time the ground was also used for speedway meetings.

Future Developments

Albion have announced their intentions to leave Cliftonhill and move to a new 3,000 capacity ground. The Club are currently investigating possible locations for the new stadium, including one at Whifflet, which is close to the site of the old Rovers ground which they played at between 1884 & 1919 before they moved to Cliftonhill. The proceeds of the sale of Cliftonhill would be used to finance the new ground.

What Is It Like For Visiting Supporters?

Crowd segregation is not in force for most games. If it is imposed then part of the Main Stand and Albion Street Terrace are given to away supporters. Stefan, a visiting fan from Germany adds; 'When I was there, they played East Stirlingshire. There was no trouble at all with visiting fans and the fans of both clubs were mixed in together in the Main Stand. The stand itself had a nice small bar at the back of it, which I enjoyed before the game. On the whole there was a very welcoming atmosphere at Cliftonhill'.

Where To Drink?

Michael Cooper informs me; 'there is a bar at the stadium itself which is aptly named 'The Rovers Return', otherwise the nearest pub to the stadium is called 'Big Owens Bar'. Away fans are welcome in both of these'. Big Owens Bar can be found further down the A89 towards Airdrie, by the fire station.

How To Get There & Where To Park?
Leave the M74 at Junction 5 at take the A725 towards Coatbridge. Continue on the A725 into the centre of Coatbridge and on reaching a large traffic island (where you can see the floodlights of the ground up on the right), turn right onto the A89 towards Airdrie. The ground is a short distance down this road on the left. Street Parking.

By Train
The nearest railway stations are Coatdyke & Whifflet, which are both about a ten-minute walk away from the ground.

Local Rivals
Airdrie United

Admission Prices

All Areas Of The Ground:
Adults £10,
Concessions £5
Children (Under 12's) Free when accompanied by a paying adult.

Programme
Official Programme £1.

Record Attendance
27,381 v Glasgow Rangers,
Scottish Cup 2nd Round, February 8th, 1936.

Average Attendance
2005-2006: 367 (Division Three)

Did You Know?
That the current floodlighting system in place at Cliftonhill, originally came from Cardiff Arms Park when it was demolished to make way for the Millennium Stadium'.

Arbroath

Gayfield Park

Ground Name: Gayfield Park
Capacity: 6,488 (seated 714)
Address: Arbroath,
Angus, DD11 1QB
Telephone No: 01241-872-157
Fax No: 01241-431-125
Pitch Size: 115 x 71 yards
Year Ground Opened: 1925*
Club Nickname: Red Lichties
Home Kit Colours: Maroon & White

Official Web Site:
www.arbroathfc.co.uk

Unofficial Websites:
Lichties News - www.arbroathfc.org.uk
Arbroath Mad (Footy Mad Network) –
www.arbroath-mad.co.uk

■ What's The Ground Like?
Gayfield is predominantly made up of terracing which extends around three corners of the ground. However, this gives the stadium a lot of character, especially as terracing is slowly but surely disappearing generally from football stadia. On one side is the new Gayfield Main Stand, opened in 2002. This is a covered single-tiered, all seated stand. The other sides of the ground are all terraces that are of a similar size. Each side has a small covered area, that covers the centre part of the terraces to the rear. There are also a number of small floodlight pylons that run down the East side of the pitch, the bases of which are situated within the East Terrace.

■ What Is It Like For Visiting Supporters?
Supporters are normally housed in the Seaforth Terrace at one end of the ground. This end is also affectionately known as the 'Pleash End' as it has the Pleasureland indoor amusement arcade at the back of it. If demand requires it, then the East Terrace at one side of the pitch can also be allocated. Normally a relaxed and hassle free day out. John Stenhouse adds; 'make sure you have a pie, they are amongst the best you'll find'.

Jamie Malley informs me; 'no matter how good the weather forecast is take a coat! and if its anytime between October and March also take a set of thermals. Gayfield is the closest ground to the sea in Britain (and in fact in Europe) and when the wind comes in off the North Sea it gets a wee bit chilly. Also if its really windy don't stand in the East terrace unless you've got an umbrella - the sea may come over the wall and you'll end up very wet!'

■ Where To Drink?
The nearest bar to the ground is the Tutties Neuk, on Queens Drive, which is just across the road from the ground. The bar is popular with both home and away fans, although it is a little on the small side.

Jamie Malley adds; 'Tutties is the place to go pre-match. Home and away supporters will freely mingle before the game and the banter is pretty good - I've even heard some away fans describe this as the best pre-match boozer in Scotland. Otherwise, within the town itself there are a number of pubs, the best of which is probably the Corn Exchange for cheap beer 'n' food. If you are after a quieter pub the harbour area has a load. For food the pies at Gayfield are so-so and if you want one best go before half time as they usually run out. Remember Arbroath is famous for its fish, so make sure you have some fish and chips before you leave. If there's a chippie that serves better and fresher fish than Peppos on the harbour, then I've yet to find it and I've eaten fish & chips all over the country! Also if you are down at the harbour there's no end of shops selling Smokies'.

■ How To Get There & Where To Park?
The ground is easy to find as it is located on the main A92. If approaching Arbroath on the A92 from the South, you will come to the ground on your right. There is plenty of street parking to be found along the sea front.

■ By Train
Arbroath train station is around a 15-minute walk away from the ground. From the railway station come out of the main entrance and turn left. Walk down to the bottom of this road and turn right into Milgate Loan. The ground is approximately half a mile along this road - you can't really miss it.

From the Bus Station - come out of the bus station onto the dual carriageway - turn right and walk away from the town towards the Signal Tower museum. You'll see the ground ahead of you - it's a 10/15-minute walk.

Thanks to Jamie Malley for providing the directions.

■ Local Rivals
Montrose, Forfar & Brechin.

■ Admission Prices
All areas of the ground

Adults - £10,
Juvenile/OAP £5.
Parent + Child £12.

■ Programme
Official Programme £1.50.

■ Record Attendance
13,510 v Rangers, February 22nd, 1952.

■ Average Attendance
2005-2006: 582 (Division Three)

■ Did You Know?
That Arbroath hold the World Record for the biggest victory in a competitive game. 36-0, against Aberdeen Bon Accord in 1885.

* The present Gayfield Park overlies part of the original Gayfield ground which dates back to 1880. The old Gayfield was demolished and the pitch moved a short distance along the coast where the new ground was built and opened in 1925.

Ground Name:	Shielfield Park
Capacity:	4,131 (Seated 1,366)
Address:	Tweedmouth,
	Berwick-upon-Tweed,
	TD15 2EF
Telephone No:	01289-307-424
Fax No:	01289-307-424
Pitch Size:	110 x 70 yards
Year Ground Opened:	1954
Club Nickname:	The Borderers
Home Kit Colours:	Gold & Black

Official Web Site:
None At Present

Unofficial Websites:
The Ducket - www.theducket.com
Berwick Rangers Mad (Footy Mad Network) -
www.berwickrangers-mad.co.uk
Berwick Rangers Online - www.berwickrangers.co.uk
Supporters Trust - www.berwickrangers.co.uk/btrust/

What's The Ground Like?
The ground is a classic oval shape, with a cinder track surrounding the playing area (which is used by the Berwick Bandits Speedway Team during the summer). Both ends are small open terraces, whilst on one side is the Main Stand. This small all seated stand is covered, but has a row of floodlights running across the front of the stand, the foundations of which could impede your view. Opposite is another mostly open terrace. However there is a small covered area, known as the 'Ducket Enclosure' which straddles the half way line.

What Is It Like For Visiting Supporters?
Supporters are not normally segregated at Shielfield. If segregation needs to be enforced then the Main Stand can be split between home and away supporters. If necessary, such as a visit by one of the old firm sides, then all of the terracing can be allocated. As Bill Purvis adds; 'Visiting supporters can enjoy a relaxed atmosphere and friendly banter both in the ground and in some of the local hostelries before the match. We do take exception however to being called "English ********" especially as most of the team and half the support are Scots'!

Where To Drink?
Nick Vagg informs me; 'There is the Black & Gold pub adjacent to the ground which is popular with both home and away fans. It has been recently refurbished and has a big screen to show Sky Sports'. Bill Purvis adds; 'Otherwise, coming into the ground by car on the B6354 (see directions) you will pass the Grove which is always popular with both sets of supporters. If you are walking from the Railway Station you will pass several pubs, most of which are not too bad, however, once you cross the River Tweed into Tweedmouth you will come upon the Angel Inn on your left which has plenty of Berwick football memorabilia adorning its walls and is a favourite haunt of the home support. After the Match many go to Barrels Alehouse, which is a well known pub situated at the Berwick end of the Old Bridge'.

How To Get There & Where To Park?

From The North:
From the A1 around Berwick and continue crossing the River Tweed. Then take the left turn towards Spittal (B6354). After about one mile, you will reach the entrance to the ground on your left.

From The South:
From the A1, take the right turn towards Spittal (B6354). After about one mile, you will reach the entrance to the ground on your left.

There is plenty of free car parking available at the ground.

By Train

Berwick station is around a twenty-minute walk away from the ground.

'As you leave the station car park, turn right and follow the road around to the left (the opposite direction to the traffic flow on a one way street). Turn right into Castlegate (this is the main road in to town). Go under the archway of the old town walls and you will come across a mini-roundabout that is opposite to the bus station. Turn right and cross the Royal Tweed Bridge. You are now in Tweedmouth. At the other end of the bridge just follow the road as it curves around to the left, passing a school and a Co-op Superstore. Just after that you will come across a railway viaduct. Turn right here into Shielfield Terrace and the ground is 150-200 yards down on your right. Thanks to Colin Wallace for providing the above directions.

Local Rivals

Bill Purvis informs me; 'Matches against Stranraer are jokingly known as Border derbies although it is probably somewhere around 190 miles between the two towns! In our present league Cowdenbeath are our main rivals'.

Admission Prices

Seating:
Adults £10,
Children & OAP's £5.

Terrace:
Adults £8,
Children & OAP's £4.

Programme
Official Programme £1.50.

Record Attendance
13,365 v Glasgow Rangers,
Scottish Cup 1st Round, January 28th, 1967.
(Berwick Won 1-0).

Average Attendance
2005-2006: 472 (Division Three)

Did You Know?
Are the only English based Club to play in the Scottish League.

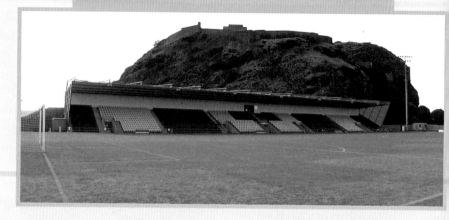

Ground Name:	Strathclyde Homes Stadium
Capacity:	2,050 (all seated)
Address:	Castle Road, Dumbarton, G82 1JJ
Telephone No:	01389-762-569
Fax No:	01389-762-629
Pitch Size:	105m x 68m
Year Ground Opened:	2000
Club Nickname:	The Sons
Home Kit Colours:	Yellow & Black

Official Web Site:
www.dumbartonfootballclub.com

Unofficial Websites:
Sons Supporters Trust - www.sonstrust.net
Dumbarton Mad (Footy Mad Network) –
www.dumbarton-ad.co.uk

What's The Ground Like?
The ground, opened in 2000, is situated spectacularly under the Castle Rock. It currently comprises one stand which sits at one side of the pitch. However the stand is of a fair size, and is covered and all-seated. The space and height between rows is ample, giving fans a good view of the action. One unusual aspect of the ground is that the team dugouts are on the opposite side of the ground to the dressing rooms and this results in a large procession at half and full time. The ground was built by Barr Construction and there is plenty of space around the area, which could be used for future expansion. David Carson adds;

'most fans refer to the ground name as being The Rock Stadium'.

What Is It Like For Visiting Supporters?
Away fans are situated in sections one and two, at one end of the new stand. Around 500 fans can be accommodated in this area. As you would expect from a new stand, the facilities are good and you should experience a hassle free day at the ground.

Where To Drink?
The nearest bar that I could find was in the Rock Bowling Club, which is just a little further down the road from the ground, opposite the entrance to the castle. Otherwise there is the Stags Head, situated opposite the entrance to East Dumbarton station. It is a good sized bar, with TVs and pool table, but unfortunately does not serve fans wearing football colours.

How To Get There & Where To Park?
Castle Rock dominates the Dumbarton skyline, and with the ground sitting just beneath, it is fairly easy to find your bearings. Follow the A814 into Dumbarton and after you go under a railway bridge, you will see a sign pointing left for Dumbarton Castle. Turn left here (Victoria Street) and the ground is down the bottom of this road on the right. There is a fair sized car park at the ground.

By Train
Dumbarton East station is only five minutes walk from the ground. As you come out of the station turn right along the main street, left into Victoria Street and the ground is down the bottom of this road on the right.

Local Rivals
Greenock Morton.

Admission Prices
Adults £10
Concessions £5

Programme
Official Programme £1.50

Record Attendance
At Strathclyde Homes Stadium:
1,959 v Queens Park,
Division Three, April 27th, 2002.

At Boghead Park:
18,000 v Raith Rovers, 1957.

Average Attendance
2005-2006: 943 (Division Two)

Did You Know?
The Club played at their previous Boghead Park
ground for 121 years; it was then Scotland's oldest
Football League Ground.

Ground Name: Bayview Stadium
Capacity: 2,000 (all seated)
Address: Harbour View, Methil, Fife, KY8 3RW
Telephone No: 01333-426-323
Fax No: 01333-426-376
Pitch Size: 115 x 75 yards
Club Nickname: Fifers
Home Kit Colours: Black & Gold

Official Web Site:
www.eastfife.org

Unofficial Websites:
East Fife History -
http://members.tripod.com/~corstorphine/historian.html
C'mon On The Fife - www.freewebs.com/effc/
Away From The Numbers - www.aftn.co.uk

What's The Ground Like?
The ground was opened in 1998, after the Club moved from its old Bayview ground. It currently has only one stand, which sits at one side of the pitch. However the stand is of a fair size, is covered and all seated. The space & height between rows is adequate, giving fans a good view of the action.

What Is It Like For Visiting Supporters?
Away fans are located in the North part of the Main Stand, where up to 1,000 can be accommodated. The facilities in this stand, as you would expect from a new ground are good, with even the stadium music and announcer piped through to the toilets! The ground is right on the coast and at times a biting wind can come off the North Sea so make sure that you wrap up well. On the down side, though, I would have to say that the outlook from this stand over the back of the ground has to be one of the ugliest I have seen at a football ground, with some huge old power station sitting beyond the grounds' perimeter.

Where To Drink?
There is a social club above the Main Stand, which welcomes away fans. It is quite a comfortable club, which enjoys views across the ground.

How To Get There & Where To Park?
The ground is quite easy to find as it is situated on the sea front and is quite visible from a distance. From Kirkcaldy take the A911 towards Methil and then the A915 to Leven. Then turn right onto the A955 towards Leven & Methil. Follow the A955 through Methil towards Buckhaven. As you go along the sea front, the ground should be visible over to your left. Turn left onto the B932 (South Street) and then left again into Harbour View Road. The ground is down the bottom of this road on the left. There is a fair sized car park at the ground.

By Train
There is no railway station in Methil itself. The nearest is in Kirkcaldy which is around eight miles away. John Thompson adds; 'On Saturdays' there is an excellent X26 bus service from Kirkcaldy to nearby Leven leaving Kirkcaldy about every 30

minutes and goes to Leven Bus station which is about 10 minutes walk from Bayview, on the other side of the old Methil Power Station. After the game there was a 17:15 X26 leaving from Leven bus station which was made no problem allowing me good time back at Kirkcaldy, that X26 actually goes back to Glasgow via Dunfermline'.

Local Rivals
Raith Rovers, Cowdenbeath.

Admission Prices

Adults - £9,
Concessions £5 (Under 15's/Over 65's).
Family Ticket - 1 Adult + 1 Child £12,
2 Adults + 2 Children £15.

Programme
Official Programme £1.

Record Attendance
At Bayview Stadium:
1,900 v Queens Park,
Division Three, May 10th, 2003.

At Bayview:
22,515 v Raith Rovers
Division One, January 2nd, 1950.

Average Attendance
2005-2006: 482 (Division Three)

Did You Know?
That East Fife is the only Second Division Club ever to win the Scottish FA Cup, which they did in 1938.

Firs Park

Ground Name: Firs Park
Capacity: 1,880 (200 Seated)
Address: Firs Street,
Falkirk, FK2 7AY
Telephone No: 01324-623-583
Fax No: 01324-637-862
Pitch Size: 112 x 72 yards
Year Ground Opened: 1921
Club Nickname: The Shire
Home Kit Colours: Black & White Hoops

Official Web Site:
www.eaststirlingshire.com

Unofficial Websites:
East Stirlingshire Mad (Footy Mad Network) –
www.eaststirlingshire-mad.co.uk
Shire Trust - http://shiretrust.netfirms.com/
Fans Forum –
www.forumage.com/index.php?mforum=shirefansforum

■ What's The Ground Like?

The ground is largely open, being predominantly terracing. One side has a small covered main stand, which is full of charm. Although it only runs for only about one third of the length of the pitch, it is of a classic design, seen at many other older grounds around the country. The seated area of this stand is elevated above the pitch, which means that spectators have to climb a set of steps to reach it. On the other side is a partly covered terrace, which unfortunately has a number of floodlight pylons running across the front of it. At one end is a larger open terrace, whilst the other end is not used. This area just has a concrete wall running the length of it, which does look somewhat out of place with the rest of the ground. As the ground is quite small a number of footballs are kicked out of the ground during the game and this keeps representatives of the club fairly busy in retrieving them.

■ Future Developments

The Club have indicated their desire to sell the present Firs Park ground for residential development and move to a new home. Whether this will mean ground sharing with another Club, such as nearby Falkirk, or moving to a new ground further away (such as Grangemouth), remains to be seen.

■ What Is It Like For Visiting Supporters?

Martin Hart, a visiting Raith fan informs me; 'There is no segregation in place at Firs Park, unless I'd imagine 'Shire were playing against local rivals. The ground is very easy to find, situated at the back of the Central Retail Park, which is full of parking spaces, and within 5 minutes walk of Firs Park, otherwise, there is limited street parking outside the ground. The nearby Central Retail Park contains a McDonalds restaurant; however, inside the ground there is a fantastic selection of food on offer, at a very reasonable price. The pies are wonderful and you can even buy homemade chicken pakora for £2. My overall verdict - A thoroughly enjoyable day out at Firs Park, which incidentally is a very tidy ground, although facilities are a little on the sparse side; other than that, a big thumbs up to East Stirlingshire from me'.

◼ Where To Drink?
A short walk from the ground is Gordons Bar & Lounge, which is popular with the supporters clubs of both home and away fans.

◼ How To Get There & Where To Park?
Follow the A904 into Falkirk. After passing Middlefield Road on your right, take the next right into Thornhill Road and then left into Firs Street for the ground.

Remember also to ignore the 'football traffic' signs around the area, as if you follow them you will eventually end up at Falkirk's ground. Street parking.

◼ By Train
The nearest station is Grahamston which is about a ten-minute walk away from the ground. As you come out of the station go left up Grahams Road and then turn right at the roundabout. Proceed through the retail park, before turning left into Victoria Road. The ground is down at the bottom of this road.

Thanks to Ben Smith for providing the directions.

◼ Local Rivals
Falkirk, Stenhousemuir.

◼ Admission Prices

All areas of the ground:
Adults £8,
Concessions £4.

◼ Programme
Official Programme 50p.

◼ Record Attendance
12,000 v Partick Thistle,
Scottish Cup, 3rd Round, February 21st, 1921.

◼ Average Attendance
2005-2006: 256 (Division Three)

◼ Did You Know?
The Club renamed itself from Bainsford Britannia to East Stirlingshire in 1881. It was the same name as a local cricket club, whose ground they took over.

Borough Briggs

Ground Name:	Borough Briggs
Capacity:	3,927 (478 Seated)
Address:	Borough Briggs Road, Elgin, IV30 1AP
Telephone No:	01343-551-114
Fax No:	01343-547-921
Pitch Size:	110 x 75 yards
Year Ground Opened:	1921
Club Nickname:	Black & Whites
Home Kit Colours:	Black & White Stripes

Official Web Site:
There isn't one at present

Unofficial Website:
Elgincity.com - www.elgincity.com

■ What's The Ground Like?

On one side of the ground is a small, covered Main Stand. This all seater stand runs for only about half the length of the pitch and straddles the half way line. There is terracing to one side of this stand. On the other side of the ground is a small, covered terrace, which is divided between home and away supporters. This enclosure looks quite old and has a number of supporting pillars. Both ends have newish open terraces that are set back from the pitch. These were opened in the year 2000. An unusual aspect of the ground is the odd-looking floodlights running down each side of the pitch, the bases of which, on the enclosure side, go down through the roof and onto the terrace, further hindering the spectators' view of the playing action.

■ What Is It Like For Visiting Supporters?

Away fans are located on the Western side of the covered enclosure. This stand is a little grim and the views of the action, unless you are right of the front of the stand can be quite poor, as there are a number of supporting pillars to contend with. The facilities in this area are quite basic, but at least it is covered and even a small number of away fans can really make some noise from this terrace. You will normally find a warm welcome at Borough Briggs and this makes for a good day out.

■ Where To Drink?

There is a supporters social club which welcomes away fans, the entrance to which is located behind the Main Stand. The social club is quite comfortable, so much so that the barman was telling me that on one occasion, two supporters from Stranraer never left the bar all Saturday afternoon and didn't get to see the game!

■ How To Get There & Where To Park?

Coming from the East or West along the A96, continue into Elgin until you reach the roundabout that has Elgin Town Hall situated on one corner. Turn at this roundabout onto the A941 (North Street) towards Lossiemouth. After a short distance down this road, take the second road on your left (Borough Briggs Road) and the ground is situated

own this road on your right. There is plenty of
street parking around the ground.

By Train

Elgin train station is about a mile from the ground
and should take about 15 minutes to walk. Kevin
Craig provides the following directions; 'As you
leave the station turn left and continue up a steep
hill. Continue straight on this road crossing two
roundabouts and at the third roundabout turn left.
Go up this road for some 500 yards and you
should see the ground on your left hand side'.

Local Rivals

Peterhead, Inverness Caledonian Thistle,
Lossiemouth & Forres.

Admission Prices

All areas of the ground

Adults £9,
Concessions £5,

Programme

Official Programme £1.

Record Attendance

12,608 v Arbroath,
Scottish Cup, February 17th, 1968.

Average Attendance

2005-2006: 429 (Division Three)

Did You Know?

The Club have played at Borough Briggs since
1921. At one time the ground was overlooked by
an old World War Two concrete pillbox. This was
demolished to make way for a new terrace in the
year 2000.

Montrose

Links Park

Ground Name: Links Park
Capacity: 3,292 (1,338 seated)
Address: Wellington St,
Montrose, DD10 8QD
Telephone No: 01674-673-200
Fax No: 01674-677-311
Pitch Size: 113 x 70 yards
Year Ground Opened: 1887
Club Nickname: The Gable Endies
Home Kit Colours: Royal Blue & White

Official Web Site:
www.montrosefc.co.uk

Unofficial Websites:
Mo Mo Super Mo (Sport Network) –
www.sportnetwork.net/main/s162.htm
Montrose Mad (Footy Mad Network) –
www.montrose-mad.co.uk
Supporters Club - www.mfcsc.com
Supporters Trust - www.gable-endies.co.uk

■ What's The Ground Like?
The ground is a largely open one, with one side
unused for spectators and one end being a small
open terrace, comprising of just six rows. The Main
Stand is a single-tiered covered stand, which is all
seated and has just over 1,300 seats. It has a
cantilever roof, meaning that there are no
supporting pillars to obstruct your view. This stand
only runs for around half the length of the pitch
and straddles the half way line. The Wellington
Street End is a small covered terrace that is a
strange looking affair. It is set well back from the
pitch, does not run the full width of it and on one
side the covered terrace kinks around towards the
pitch itself, but not around the corner flag as you
would expect. Whether this was designed to help

protect the fans against the prevailing wind I don't
know, but it certainly looks odd. There are also a
row of supporting pillars in this end, plus a small
fence that runs across the front of it. The ground is
completed with a set of four modern looking
floodlight pylons, one in each corner.

■ What Is It Like For Visiting Supporters?
Normally segregation is not in force at Links Park.
However, if it is enforced, then half the Main Stand
(around 700 seats) is allocated, with away fans
also being allowed to stand around the perimeter
of the ground, on the two sides that are normally
unused. Links Park is normally a good day out,
the pies are great, however at times the ground
lacks a little in atmosphere.

Jon Blackwood adds; 'Links Park rarely sees
crowds of more than 500 these days, although
Montrose could count on 800-1000 in their days
in the first division. Pre-season friendlies against
Aberdeen and Dundee United, and derby games
against Arbroath, always attract four-figure crowds.
Other than the odd lively atmosphere for derby
games against Montrose's bitter rivals, Arbroath,
there is never, ever any trouble and the home fans
are friendly. There's not a huge amount to do in
Montrose but if its a sunny early or end of season
game the beach is great and it's worth looking at
the distinctive Auld Kirk building'.

■ Where To Drink?
Douglas Walker informs me; 'The nearest bar is the
Golf Inn on Mill Street. It is only a five-minute walk
away from the ground'. Whilst John Laidlaw adds;
'There is a British Legion Club near to the
turnstiles, that from a distance looks more like a
house rather than a Club (there is a small yellow
sign attached to a wall above the entrance). It will
sometimes allow non-members to be signed in,
which is worth the effort as it serves a cracking

pint'. Otherwise if you are walking from the train station then the Corner House Hotel next to the Auld Kirk is worth a visit.

■ How To Get There & Where To Park?
The ground is signposted from the A92, as you enter the town.

From The North:
Take the A92 into Montrose. Just as the road turns towards the seafront, turn left into Rosehill Road. Take the 4th right into Warrack Terrace and then third left into Wellington Street for the ground.

From The South
Take the A92 to the outskirts of Montrose. Turn right into Wharf Street (B9133 signposted 'Football Traffic') and then bear left into Hill Street. Continue straight on up this road going over a crossroads into Panmore Place (sign posted Sports Centre). Follow this road passing the Town Hall on your right and then as you run alongside a small strip of park on your right, you should be able to see the floodlights of the ground just beyond it. Turn right into Wellington Street for the ground.

There is a fair-sized car park at the ground, otherwise street parking.

■ By Train
Montrose railway station is approximately one mile away from Links Park and should take around 15 minutes to walk. From the train station, cross over the Somerfield Car park and head towards the spire of the Auld Kirk. Turn left onto Hume Street, then left again onto the High Street. Cross the road, then right down John Street. Keep straight ahead, crossing over Mill Street and Provost Scott Road. Turn left up Eastern Road, then right when you come to Wellington Street. You'll see the home turnstiles straight ahead of you. Otherwise a taxi from the station up to the ground should cost about £3. Thanks to Jon Blackwood for providing the above directions.

■ Local Rivals
Arbroath, Forfar & Brechin City.

■ Admission Prices

Seating:
Adults £7.50,
Concessions £4.

Terrace:
Adults £7,
Concessions £3.50.

■ Programme
Official Programme £1.50.

■ Record Attendance
8,983 v Dundee, Scottish Cup 3rd Round, March 17th, 1973.

■ Average Attendance
2005-2006: 422 (Division Three)

■ Did You Know?
That the Club nickname of Gable Endies, has its origins in the local architecture of Montrose, where many buildings have the gable end exposed onto the street.

Ground Name: Hampden Park
Capacity: 52,500 (all seated)
Address: Mount Florida, Glasgow, G42 9BA
Telephone No: 0141-632-1275
Fax No: 0141-636-1612
Pitch Size: 115 x 75 yards
Year Ground Opened: 1903
Club Nickname: Spiders
Home Kit Colours: Black & White

Official Web Site:
www.queensparkfc.co.uk

Unofficial Website:
Queen's Park Fansite - www.queensparkfansite.cjb.net

■ What's The Ground Like?

The stadium has been completely redeveloped in recent years and the predominantly old terraced ground has now been transformed into a modern all-seated stadium. Although not particularly large for a national stadium, it still retains its charm and individual character which is enhanced by its completely enclosed oval shape. Three sides of the stadium are single-tiered, but the South Stand on one side of it, has a small second tier, which slightly overhangs the lower one. Normally this may mean that the stadium would look imbalanced, but it has been well integrated with the rest of the stadium with the oval stadium roof rising gently towards this stand. There are also two electric scoreboards which are suspended underneath the roofs at either end of the stadium.

One unusual aspect of the stadium is that the team dugouts are actually situated six rows up on the South Stand. This is to allow team managers to get a better view of the game.

■ What Is It Like For Visiting Supporters?

Only part of the BT Scotland South Stand is open for Queens Park games and normally segregation of fans is not enforced. Two turnstiles (P & O) which are open for each game are located to the left of the main entrance. If segregation is in force, then away fans use turnstiles I & J, which are located to the right of the main entrance.

The facilities within Hampden are great, plus the leg room and view of the playing action, are also both good. On the good sized concourse there is a small club shop and refreshments on sale include; Steak Pie (£1.90), Scotch Pie (£1.40), Macaroni Pie (£1.70), Cheeseburger (£2.70) & Chips.

Although a pleasant afternoon out, crowds of around the 5-600 mark, in a 52,500-seater stadium, does little for the atmosphere. In fact, at times, you would be thinking that you were attending a reserve match, with the players' voices echoing around the ground. Still, the PA system booms around the stadium before the game and at half time, the electric scoreboards are in operation and there is still a game of football to be watched.

On my last visit against Albion Rovers, five minutes before kick-off, there was a fair queue for refreshments. An Albion fan shouts to his friend in the queue; 'Hurry up Willie, or else we'll not get a seat!'. That brought a smile to my face considering that there were around 52,000 empty seats inside the stadium.

Queens Park

■ Where To Drink?
There is the Queens Park Social Club, in Somerville Drive (adjacent in office accommodation to the nearby Lesser Hampden ground), which allows in away fans. Otherwise there are a number of bars and chippies around the area of the stadium. My favourite is the Clockwork Beer Company on Cathcart Road (going away from the city centre). This spacious pub brews its own beers and stocks a wide range of whiskies.

■ How To Get There & Where To Park?

From The M8/M73/M74:
Leave the M74 at Junction 1 and turn left at the roundabout into Fullarton Road, following the signs for Rutherglen. Go straight across the next roundabout and at the following roundabout turn right into Cambuslang Road. You will cross over the River Clyde and then continue to the end of this road. At the traffic lights turn right and continue along Main Street Rutherglen and then on towards Mount Florida. Continue straight along this road until you reach the large Asda Store at which you turn left into Aikenhead Road. The stadium is up this road on the right hand side. There is a large free car park, behind the South Stand.

■ By Train
The nearest stations to the stadium are Mount Florida & Kings Park. Both are served by trains from Glasgow Central (journey time around 10-15 minutes) and are around a five-minute walk away from the stadium.

■ Local Rivals
Clyde & Albion Rovers.

■ Admission Prices

Adults £9,
Concessions £2.
Parent plus up to 4 Children - £10
(£1 per extra child thereafter).

■ Programme
Official Programme £2.

■ Record Attendance
For Hampden:
149,415 - Scotland v England, 1937.
This is the record for the largest attendance at a football match in Britain.

For Queens Park:
95,722 v Rangers (1930).

■ Average Attendance
2005-2006: 506 (Division Three)

■ Other Places Of Interest
For all those ground enthusiasts out there, then make sure you take a peak at the old lesser Hampden, behind the West Stand. This is a small old ground, that has quite a quaint-looking stand at one side of the pitch. In the past it has been used by Queens Park reserves, as well as for the odd first team outing.

The stadium is also the home of the Scottish Football Museum, which opened its doors in May 2001. I was thoroughly impressed not only with the standard of museum, but also the vast array of items that can be seen. From a ticket from the first ever Football International held in Glasgow in 1872, to an exhibition of football related 'toys'. The current Scottish Cup is also available to view within the museum.

What I particularly liked was the emphasis on the fans' involvement in the Clubs, from the first fanzines to the Tartan Army. The museum is a must for any true football supporter.

The museum is open daily from 10.00am to 5pm (Sunday's 11am-5pm, Last admittance all days - 4.15pm). Entrance costs £5.50 for adults and £2.75 for concessions. Tours of the stadium are also available on non matchdays for an additional charge of £3 adults, £1.75 concessions. Alternatively if you wish you can just book a tour of the stadium which costs £6 adults, £3 concessions. If you have an enquiry you can ring the museum on 0141-616-6139. Queens Park offer on matchdays a joint 'museum entry and matchday' ticket for just £10.

■ Did You Know?
That Queens Park are Scotland's oldest football league club, having been formed in 1867.

Stenhousemuir

Ochilview Park

Ground Name: Ochilview Park
Capacity: 5,267 (2,117 Seated)
Address: Gladstone Rd,
Stenhousemuir, FK5 4QL
Telephone No: 01324-562-992
Fax No: 01324-562-980
Pitch Size: 110 x 72 yards
Year Ground Opened: 1890
Club Nickname: Warriors
Home Kit Colours: Maroon & White

Official Web Site:
www.stenhousemuirfc.com

Unofficial Websites:
Norwegian Supporters Club - www.stenhousemuir.com
Stenhousemuir Mad (Footy Mad Network) –
www.stenhousemuir-mad.co.uk

■ What's The Ground Like?
On one side of the ground is the relatively new-
looking Main Stand (also known by the locals as
the McCowans End, after the toffee factory in the
same street). This small, all-seated, covered stand,
runs for about half the length of the pitch and
straddles the half way line. It has a couple of
floodlights perched on its roof. Opposite to this
stand the side of the ground is unused for
spectators and just has the team dugouts and a
row of small floodlights. At the Tryst Road End of
the ground is a good-sized terrace that has

recently had a roof put on it, giving much needed
shelter for the standing fans. On one side of this
terrace can be seen a Social Club which is owned
by the Club. The opposite East End of the ground is
again unused for spectators.

■ What Is It Like For Visiting Supporters?
Generally there is no segregation of fans for league
games. If segregation needs to be enforced, then
away fans are predominantly housed in the
covered Tryst Road terrace which is allocated
specifically to them, whilst some seats are also
allocated in the Main Stand. Normally a friendly
welcome awaits the visiting supporter and I
experienced no problems on my visit.

■ Where To Drink?
There is a Social Club on one corner of the Tryst
Road terrace and a small bar under the Main
Stand. Both welcome away supporters, although
on occasions the Social Club may charge a small
entrance fee, for non members. There are a couple
of bars to be found in the nearby town centre
(five minutes walk).

■ How To Get There & Where To Park?
Leave the M876 at Junction 2 and follow the A88
towards Stenhousemuir. After about three quarters
of a mile turn right into Tryst Road. The ground is
down the bottom of this road on the left. It is not
the easiest ground to spot as it has no large
floodlights that can be seen from a distance.
Remember also to ignore the 'football traffic' signs

around the area, as if you follow them you will eventually end up at Falkirk's ground. Street parking.

By Train
The nearest train station is Larbert, which is about half a mile away from the ground. As you come out of the station, bear left down the main (King Street) road in front of the station. Continue down Kings Road and you will reach the ground on the left.

Local Rivals
Falkirk, Stirling Albion & Alloa.

Admission Prices

Seating:
Adults £9,
Concessions £5.

Terrace:
Adults £6,
Concessions £4.

Programme
Official Programme £1.20.

Record Attendance
12,500 v East Fife, March 11th, 1950.
Scottish Cup 4th Round.

Average Attendance
2005-2006: 475 (Division Three)

Did You Know?
The first modern floodlit game in Scotland was played at Ochilview in 1951, when the Club played Hibernian in a friendly.

Capacity: 52,500 (all seated)
Address: Letherby Drive, Glasgow, G42 9BA

Scottish Football Association (SFA):
Telephone No: 0141-616-6000
Fax No: 0141-616-6001
Pitch Size: 115 x 75 yards
Year Stadium Opened: 1903

Official Stadium Web Site:
www.hampdenpark.co.uk
SFA Website: www.scottishfa.co.uk
Scottish Football Museum:
www.scottishfootballmuseum.org.uk

■ What's The Stadium Like?

Hampden has been completely redeveloped in recent years and the old, predominantly terraced ground has now been transformed into a modern all seated stadium. Although not particularly large for a national stadium, it still retains its charm and individual character, enhanced by its completely enclosed oval shape. Three sides are single-tiered, but the South Stand on one side has a small second tier, which slightly overhangs the lower one. Normally this creates an unbalanced look, but it has integrated well with the oval stadium roof rising gently towards this stand. There are two electric scoreboards suspended underneath the roofs at each end. One unusual aspect of the stadium is that the team dugouts are actually situated six rows up on the South Stand, allowing team managers to get a better view of the game. The roof of the stadium is adorned with a number of flagpoles and flags, adding to the overall occasion.

With Rangers & Celtic both contesting a number of finals at the stadium, it has now become traditional for each team to be allotted the same ends. So Celtic are allocated the East End of the stadium and Rangers the West End.

The stadium is also the home of Queens Park FC, who are the only amateur club to compete in the Scottish Football League. Hampden is also occasionally used as a concert venue.

■ What Is It Like For Visiting Supporters?

The facilities are pretty good. The concourse is spacious and there is a good selection of food on offer including the 'Hampden Steak Pie' (£1.90), burgers, chips and hot dogs. There are televisions next to the serving areas showing the game being played inside, so that you don't have to miss a kick. There are also Ladbrokes betting facilities available. One tip, if the queues for programmes are quite big outside the stadium, then you can purchase them from programme sellers on the concourse inside.

Fans are set well back from the playing action as there is a quite a gap between the first rows of seats and the pitch. If you are at the back of the ends then this is even more noticeable as you are quite far from the pitch, meaning that you may struggle to see the action at the opposite end. This is not helped by the shallow incline of the stands, which may mean that your view is less than perfect. If possible, it is probably best to obtain tickets in either the North or South Stands, where the views are better. However, the leg room between rows is good, plus the atmosphere generated within the stadium and the colourful display by the supporters can be superb.

David Tennant, a visiting St Mirren supporter adds; 'the selection of grub available inside the stadium was impressive. The pies were great and I loved the hamburgers they sold. There are also betting facilities available which is good if you fancy a late wee flutter. The atmosphere generated by the place was, despite its very wide bowl shape, very impressive too'.

■ Where To Drink?
There are not a great number of bars in the immediate vicinity of the stadium. What ones there can get overcrowded. It is, therefore, probably best to drink in the City Centre or en route to the game. There are, though, a number of chippies/kebab shops locally. If you do get there early then my favourite bar in the area is the Clockwork Beer Company on Cathcart Road (going away from the city centre). This spacious pub brews its own varied selection of beers and also stocks a wide range of whiskies; or more affectionately known as the 'water of life'.

■ How To Get There & Where To Park?
Leave the M74 at Junction 1 and turn left at the roundabout into Fullarton Road, following the signs for Rutherglen. Go straight across the next roundabout and at the following roundabout turn right into Cambuslang Road. You will cross over the River Clyde and then continue to the end of this road. At the traffic lights turn right and continue along Main Street Rutherglen and then on towards Mount Florida. Continue straight along this road until you reach the large Asda Store at which you turn left into Aikenhead Road. The stadium is up this road on the right hand side.

David Tennant adds 'It is not straightforward to get to by road and it's not easy to get parked for a big match. So allow plenty of time for your journey'. Parking spaces can typically be found in the area around the Victoria Infirmary'.

■ By Train
The nearest stations to the stadium are Mount Florida & Kings Park. Both are served by trains from Glasgow Central (journey time around 10-15 minutes) and are around a five-minute walk away from the stadium.

■ International Matches
For International Matches visiting supporters are housed in the South West corner of the stadium (including a small portion of the upper tier of the South Stand) where around 3,000 supporters can be accommodated. Please note that in common with other Scottish Grounds, alcohol is not available inside the stadium, nor is smoking permitted within the stadium. The 'Tartan Army of Scottish supporters' are renowned for their friendliness and hospitality, which normally makes for a great visit.

■ Scottish Football Museum
The stadium is also the home of the Scottish Football Museum, which opened its doors in May 2001. I was thoroughly impressed not only with the standard of the museum, but also the vast array of items that can be seen, from a ticket from the first ever Football International held in Glasgow in 1872, to an exhibition of football related 'toys'. The current Scottish Cup is also available to view within the museum.

What I particularly liked was the emphasis on the fans involvement in the Clubs, from the first fanzines to the Tartan Army. The museum is a must for any true football supporter.

The museum is open daily from 10.00am to 5pm (Sunday's 11am-5pm, Last admittance all days - 4.15pm). Entrance costs £5.50 for adults and £2.75 for concessions. If you have an enquiry you can ring the museum on 0141-616-6139. A visit to the museum can also be combined with a tour of the stadium (see below).

■ Stadium Tours
Stadium tours are available each day (except matchdays) for the bargain price of £3 adults and

£1.75 for concessions, if booked in conjunction with an entrance ticket to the museum. If you just want to book the stadium tour only then this costs £6 for adults and £3 for concessions. Family tickets are also available, giving further discounts. The tour lasts about 40 minutes and includes the Presentation Area, Dressing Rooms, Warm Up Area and a walk at pitch side. I found it quite entertaining and interesting, and would recommend it. Tours can be booked in advance on 0141-616-6139.

■ Other Places Of Interest

For all those ground enthusiasts out there, then make sure you take a peek at the lesser Hampden, behind the West Stand. This is a small old ground with a quaint looking stand at one side of the pitch. In the past it has been used by Queens Park reserves, as well as for the odd first team outing.

Of equal, if not more interest, are the remnants of another ground called Cathkin Park, home to Third Lanark until 1967, when they unfortunately went out of business. The ground was originally built in 1872 and once hosted an international match in 1884, between Scotland and England. There is plenty of terracing still remaining of the old ground, in a picturesque setting and it is only a ten-minute walk away from the present Hampden. The entrance to the park is in Cathcart Road, down on the right past Mount Florida train station.

■ Record Attendance

149,415 - Scotland v England, 1937.
This is the record for the largest attendance at a football match in Britain.

■ Did You Know?

That until 1950, Hampden Park, with a capacity of 150,000 was the world's largest football ground.

Ground Plans

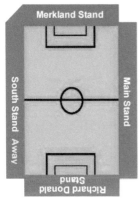

Aberdeen

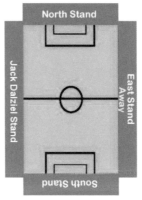

Airdrie United

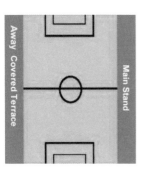

Albion Rovers

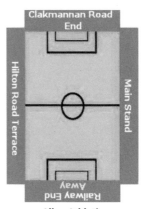

Alloa Athletic

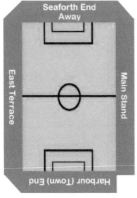

Arbroath

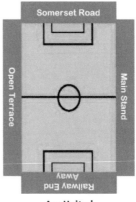

Ayr United

Ground Plans

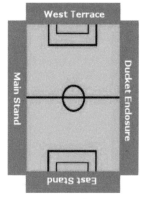

Berwick

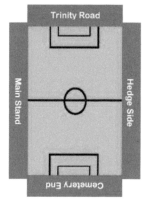

Brechin City

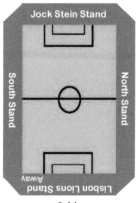

Celtic

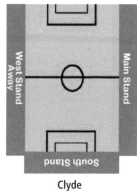

Clyde

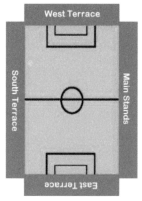

Cowdenbeath

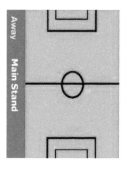

Dumbarton

Ground Plans

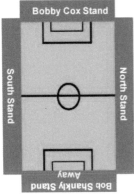

Dundee

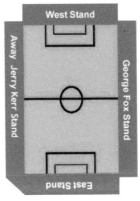

Dundee United

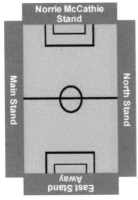

Dunfermline

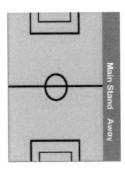

East Fife

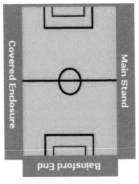

East Stirlingshire

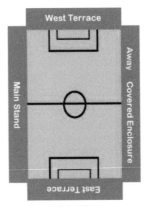

Elgin City

Ground Plans

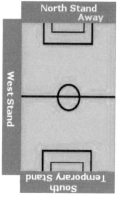

Falkirk

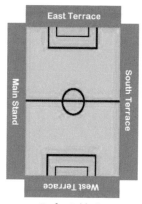

Forfar Athletic

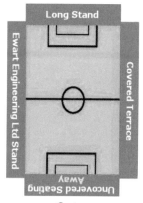

Gretna

Hamilton Academical

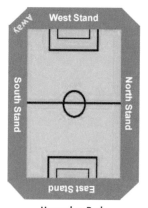

Hampden Park

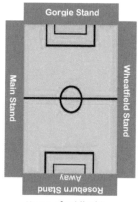

Heart of Midlothian

Ground Plans

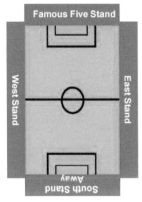

Hibernian

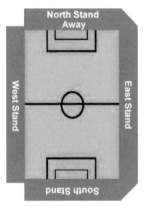

Inverness Caledonian Thistle

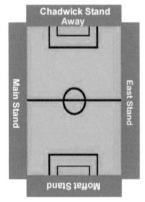

Kilmarnock

Livingston

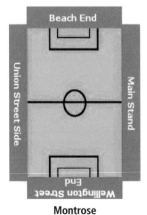

Montrose

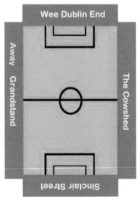

Morton

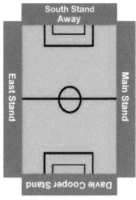

Motherwell

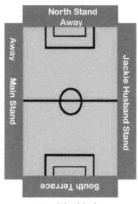

Partick Thistle

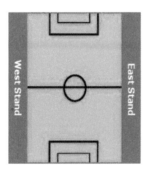

Peterhead

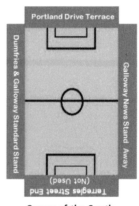

Queen of the South

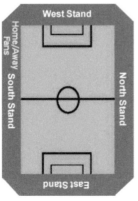

Queens Park

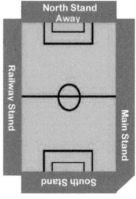

Raith Rovers

Ground Plans

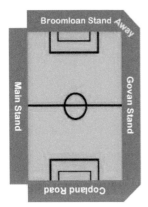

Rangers

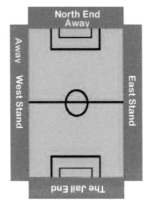

Ross County

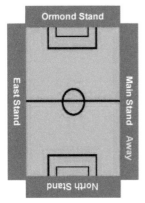

St Johnstone

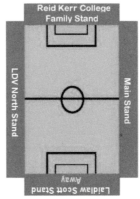

St Mirren

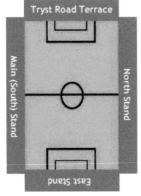

Stenhousemuir

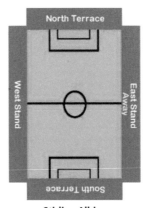

Stirling Albion

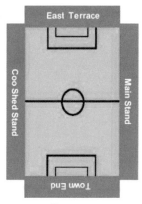

Stranraer